Just for the Money?

What really motivates us at work

Adrian Furnham
with Tom Booth

CYAN

Marshall Cavendish
Business

Copyright © 2005 Adrian Furnham and Tom Booth

First published in 2005 by:

Marshall Cavendish Business
An imprint of Marshall Cavendish International (Asia) Private Limited
A member of Times Publishing Limited
Times Centre, 1 New Industrial Road
Singapore 536196
T: +65 6213 9300
F: +65 6285 4871
E: te@sg.marshallcavendish.com
Online bookstore: www.marshallcavendish.com/genref

and

Cyan Communications Limited
119 Wardour Street
London W1F 0UW
United Kingdom
www.cyanbooks.com

A CIP record for this book is available from the British Library

ISBN 981 261 819 8 (Asia & ANZ)
ISBN 1-904879-50-0 (Rest of world)

Printed and bound in Singapore

Contents

Figures and tables

FIGURES

TABLE

Preface

Money is such a preoccupation in our lives today. We labor under the disillusion that it will make us happy. The lack of it certainly has the power to make us unhappy. But if you think it is the route to solving all your problems and eternal happiness, think again.

The topic of money is charged. We find it difficult to talk about. Indeed, as Adrian and Tom point out, couples find it easier to talk about sex than they do to talk about money. We are preoccupied with it, we worry about it, we become obsessed that others have more than us, and we use it to indicate our status and our values.

Some people treat the acquisition of money as an end in itself, not as a means to an end. For these people there is never enough. They may have an idea that one day they will be able to stop striving—one day they will have enough, but the reality is they won't. They don't know when to stop because enough is never enough.

Money can be such an indicator of our psychological story. Adrian and Tom explore how our childhood and the role models we had when we were younger shape the way we relate to money for the rest of our lives. People's behavior when it comes to money is determined by the messages they were given as children.

It's astonishing then that in the world of work the whole treatment of financial reward is governed by economics and is based on economic theory.

Like much of what we do in organizational life, when it comes to money we rarely question our deeply held assumptions. We think that we can pay to get better performance. As in other aspects of managing people we try to simplify the complex. We assume that human beings are rational and we assume that they are driven and motivated by the same things. It is these assumptions that lead universal pay and incentive systems for all. Companies spend vast amounts of money and time designing and running pay and incentives systems. These pay systems don't take account of the fact that people are different and are motivated by different things. And they rarely do what they are intended to do: get people to work harder or produce more.

Adrian and Tom do a great job of exploding the myths about money and the effect it has on people in the workplace. It's a complex business. They make it easy to understand. They also make it obvious that the key to motivating people and encouraging them to give their all to the job is not through money. Most people, provided they feel fairly paid and well treated, do not work harder, show more loyalty, or do their jobs with more commitment and passion just because they have the carrot of more pay or a bonus. People do a good job because of the intrinsic rewards that they get from doing so. The days of doing a job just for the money are gone. People are increasingly looking for meaning in their work lives. More meaning does not come from earning more; it comes from loving what you do.

Companies would do well to pay some attention to finding ways of helping people to find more fulfillment in their work, not to relentlessly beating the "executive compensation" drum. What is more, those people who respond to the promise of more financial rewards are not the ones who are likely to be able to take their companies forward into the new-enlightened age. Passion, commitment, and creativity need nurturing and find fulfillment with kindred spirits and in meaningful work environments. Those who chase bigger pay packets and bonuses are those who inhabit the "set the targets high, cut the costs" school of management. Sure, there are many successful businesses built on this way of doing things, but the companies who, over the next 20 years, will rise to the top on all measures of success, not just financial ones, will be the ones that really understand that it is attachment to certain values that will attract the people who will create success. It is not the promise of fat pay checks.

Sally Bibb
Series Editor

1

The importance of money

INTRODUCTION

This book is predicated on four fundamental, evidence-based truths.

1. Most people are far from rational with respect to money. People can be, and are all too frequently, *irrational* and *a-rational* about their money. This is because money is deeply imbued with symbolic meaning. Our attitudes to, beliefs about, and decisions concerning money have psychological meaning and are understandable. But they rarely follow economic or rational logic. Economists are often simply wrong because they describe how people *should* rather than *do* behave. Clever, educated, supposedly rational people simply do not behave as economic models say they should.
2. Our attitudes to beliefs about our spending and saving of money have much to do with our childhood and early education. A significant number of "money troubled" people can trace problems to messages they got in early life. More people are money troubled than you think: they are, and know they are, irrational savers, profligate spenders, and anti-social misers. Their money habits can and do wreck relationships and cause serious problems at work. These problems can be treated but they need to be recognized first.
3. At work, money is a powerful *de*motivator, rather than a powerful motivator. There is quite simply a very weak relationship between pay and productivity, and pay and satisfaction, over the long term. But there is a very strong relationship between money and morale.

And what we know is this—money can decrease motivation or at least change it. It can shift attention from quality to quantity; from intrinsic to extrinsic; from "we" to "me." If people feel unfairly rewarded (pay being part of the reward package) with respect to others inside *and* outside of the work organization, they can easily and quickly become angry, disloyal, and demotivated. They are quickly able to adapt to increases in pay, which makes money a very expensive and addictive way to attempt to boost morale. Further, satisfaction with pay is more a function of the perception of comparative fairness than the actual amount received. And, people are often quite happy to trade off money for pay.

4. Money and well-being are only tangentially related. In short, money cannot buy happiness. It certainly can in some instances prevent types of unhappiness but it can't, per se, be an easy solution to life's problems. By understanding what factors do lead to happiness and satisfaction in life and at work, we can better understand why money and happiness are poorly linked. It also explains why money is not as important as many other factors relating to work and motivation and productivity.

Few social scientists would dispute the above. Even economists are coming round to accepting the data about money and happiness, money and morale at work, and decision making about money.

Alas, many people at work are not so wise. They like to hold on to old myths and re-chant many mantras. Part of the problem is that money is, at once, both a fascinating and a taboo topic.

Yet money is a very frequent topic of conversation. The media are full of money talk: it appears in all the pages of newspapers, not just the financial pages. People talk about taxes, house prices, about inflation and the stock market, as well as about the salaries of public figures and the cost of private health. Money is a powerful influence.

But there are written and unwritten rules and codes about these conversations. You may ask what people paid for a car but not a house; for furniture but not a dress; for a flight but not a holiday. It has been suggested that a young liberated couple who might have sex on their first date find it easier to agree on the sex than who pays the bill for dinner or the taxi back for "coffee."

While these "rules" may differ from person to person, social class to social class, culture to culture, and time to time, it probably does remain true that some money topics are completely taboo in nearly every culture. For most people it is quite unacceptable to discuss precisely how much they earn; how much they have saved; how much tax they pay; what they have left in their will; or what they would be prepared to do for a large sum of money.

Money talk is not easy. It is full of traps, hidden rules, and sources of embarrassment. In short, money talk remains a curious and stubborn social taboo. And this has consequences. It can, and does, happen that not being too open and honest about money beliefs and behaviors during courtship can lead a couple to serious disagreements and fights during marriage, and then in due course to attempts to financially humiliate and destroy each other during divorce.

A simple but effective illustration of the power of the symbolism and of the complexity of money is the way we talk about it in everyday life. Consider the intoxicating, maddening, inflaming aspect of money:

> There is blood-money, bride-money, conscience money and stolen money, easy money and money that has been earned by the sweat of the brow, money to burn and money as the prize of merit; there is money that is a king's ransom and money that is a whore's pay; there is money to squander and so much money as will make it difficult for its possessor to get into heaven. There is the mistress's allowance and the wife's due; pocket-money, spending money, hush money, and money in the bank; there are the wages of sin and the bequests of rich uncles; there is the price that every man has, and the pricelessness of objects and the price on the outlaw's head; there are the forty pieces of silver and also the double indemnity on one's own life.
>
> (Wiseman 1974, p15)

Money can thus be associated with:

> armour, ardour, admiration, freedom, power and authority, excitement and elation, insulation, survival and security, sexual potency, victory and reward. Thus, money may be perceived as a weapon or shield, a sedative or a stimulant, a talisman or an aphrodisiac, a satisfying morsel of food or a warm fuzzy blanket...so having money in our pockets, to save or to spend, may provide us with feelings of fullness, warmth, pride, sexual attractiveness, invulnerability, perhaps even immortality. Similarly, experiencing a dearth of money may bring on

feelings of emptiness, abandonment, diminishment, vulnerability, inferiority, impotency, anxiety, anger and envy.

(Matthews 1991, p.24)

Attitudes to money come from four different sources:

1. *Childhood*: How one's parents and family talked and thought about money; their actual financial situation; and their polymorphous perversity (many formed oddities) with respect to money.
2. *Education and media:* What one is taught outside the family, both at school (university) and in the workplace, particularly in early jobs.
3. *Social comparison*: How frequently and who people compare themselves to in terms of income, savings, possessions.
4. *Community/society*: All sorts of social forces like inflation, growth, depression, war, can have a profound effect on jobs and therefore money.

Wilson (1999, p.183) notes the symbolism and associates of money in Figure 1.1.

Parents as well as cultures, and whole societies, send frequent, subtle, even mixed money messages. They define what it means to be rich or poor; how money should be made or stored; how "disposable income" should be spent; how to show off or conceal your money. Society dictates who are money heroes and anti-heroes.

Societal values dictate what "economics" should be taught in class. It dictates what financial and other advertisements are allowed on the television. It prescribes and proscribes how one deals with charity. Charities are

FIGURE 1.1 EVERYDAY MONEY LANGUAGE

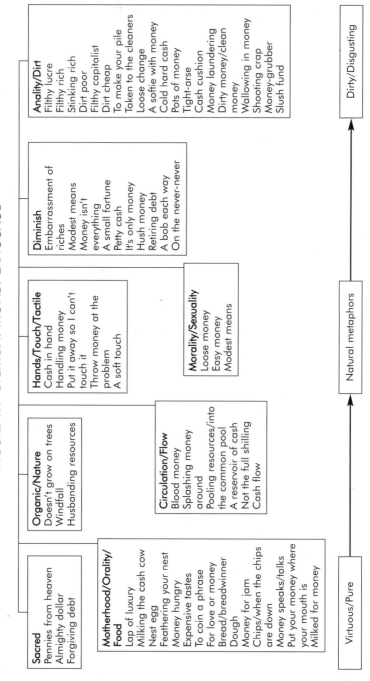

Sacred
Pennies from heaven
Almighty dollar
Forgiving debt

Organic/Nature
Doesn't grow on trees
Windfall
Husbanding resources

Hands/Touch/Tactile
Cash in hand
Handling money
Put it away so I can't touch it
Throw money at the problem
A soft touch

Diminish
Embarrassment of riches
Modest means
Money isn't everything
A small fortune
Petty cash
It's only money
Hush money
Retiring debt
A bob each way
On the never-never

Anality/Dirt
Filthy lucre
Filthy rich
Stinking rich
Dirt poor
Filthy capitalist
Dirt cheap
To make your pile
Taken to the cleaners
Loose change
A softie with money
Cold hard cash
Pots of money
Tight-arse
Cash cushion
Money laundering
Dirty money/clean money
Wallowing in money
Shooting crap
Money-grubber
Slush fund

Motherhood/Orality/Food
Lap of luxury
Milking the cash cow
Nest egg
Feathering your nest
Money hungry
Expensive tastes
To coin a phrase
For love or money
Bread/breadwinner
Dough
Money for jam
Chips/when the chips are down
Money speaks/talks
Put your money where your mouth is
Milked for money

Circulation/Flow
Blood money
Splashing money around
Pooling resources/into the common pool
A reservoir of cash
Not the full shilling
Cash flow

Morality/Sexuality
Loose money
Easy money
Modest means

Virtuous/Pure ———→ Natural metaphors ———→ Dirty/Disgusting

becoming psychologically very sophisticated when it comes to money. They understand how to "tug the heart strings," induce guilt, and maximize spontaneous spur-of-the-moment giving.

People learn money attitudes in the home, at school, and at work. Some believe it is more important to have a job they like rather than one that pays well. Others will sacrifice intrinsic for extrinsic motivation. That is, they will do difficult, stressful, even demeaning and dirty work for substantial rewards. They are willing to sacrifice job satisfaction, fun, the feeling of *flow*, simply for money. Some believe that rich people work harder than poor people, which explains why they are successful. Others believe privilege and corruption are more likely to account for the riches of the wealthy than work. Some believe there is nothing morally wrong about going into debt. Others believe it is almost sinful. Some feel that "good" people never spend money on themselves but only on their friends and family. Others believe the self-sacrificial stand to be misguided and hypocritical.

All therapists are eager to debunk modern myths about money: specifically about what money is not. All this despite the fact that, quite clearly, money is clearly a great aphrodisiac: see the number of elderly (relatively unattractive) millionaires with very much younger trophy wives. Money gives people the opportunity to exercise choice (where to live and work; how to travel). Money can give people status and authority, depending on how it was obtained. Money myths prevail everywhere. The argument is that each myth contains a *kernel of truth* but is actually wrong.

- *Money equals happiness*: Often the most pleasurable experiences/activities take little money. There are many very contented, happy, non-rich people and vice versa.

■ *Money brings love*: As all shopaholics know, money cannot substitute for love or make one more lovable.

■ *Money gives people power*: It does not bring personal power, but it may bring only negative power. It can't buy real friendship.

■ *Money buys freedom*: Maybe, but it cannot buy health.

■ *Money increases self-worth*: Self-respect, self-esteem do not arise (solely) from money. Nor indeed do people respect others because of their money (however acquired).

■ *Money brings security*: What brings security is good relationships and social support, not money.

MONEY MESSAGES AT WORK

Just as parents send powerful explicit money messages, so do organizations. They give messages about abundance and scarcity; about equality and equity-based distribution; about fairness and cheating customers. Nearly all people want to be happy at work: to feel energized, proud, respected, and valued. They want to feel they are making a real contribution and exploiting their talents. They also want to work with people they like and value.

Most organizations are happy to set out their corporate values through such things as vision and mission statements. The issues to consider are, however:

■ Whether expressed corporate values are "lived out" in corporate behavior or whether they are simply a bit of wishful thinking. Indeed it could be that stated corporate values are the very opposite of how senior managers behave in the organization. They talk about customer care but are only interested in profit. They stress quality but pay attention to quantity.

■ Whether there is a happy fit between corporate and personal values. It could be that there is a slight or severe misfit that could have serious repercussions.

Business sends conflicting messages, as do individuals. Private versus public sector; big versus small; national versus international businesses—all have different values. People look over the fence, often happy to entertain unproven stereotypes—such as that people in the public sector are lazy, risk-averse, customer-unresponsive jobsworths, or that people in the private sector are avaricious, uncaring, and materialistic.

It is no doubt very different working for a not-for-profit charity or public sector organization as opposed to an expanding profit-making business. The former might rely on praise and thanks, and the latter on pay, to motivate.

This book is about how attitudes, beliefs, and behaviors are associated with money. Specifically it concentrates on money at work. It hopes to confront the myths and half-truths about the motivational power of money.

Money is a medium of exchange and legal tender, but it is deeply and complexly *symbolic*. Everybody except, paradoxically, economists knows what money means and represents.

Most people recognize that money has a childhood. Money secrecy begins then. Children discover that money is emotionally evocative, that it is a mystery but that it is also closely linked to morality. Children learn and retain money maxims. Memories about money matter; they cloud, taunt, and influence all adult money-related behavior. So one can become a prude about money, or indeed prurient. Many of us are captives of our past. Even well-educated, clever adults can be shown to make frequent less-than-rational decisions about their money.

People have to control their money. The words they use are management, budgeting, and organizing, but it is really about control. And control is closely linked to power (Wilson 1999).

TRADE-OFFS AND MONEY

What is money worth? What are you prepared to do for money? How much are you prepared to compromise your principles, break the law, and bring shame on your family simply for money? Think of your job: What would you be prepared to do for a raise of £10,000? How much stress, responsibility, and accountability would you be prepared to take? What, anyway, would you do with the money?

The British, it is said, are masters of compromise. The act of compromising can be seen as positive or negative, weak or strong, pusillanimous or practical. In a negative light, we talk of "compromising our principles" or "compromising the strategy." It means that we settle for less than best; we give up on our original (explicit) plans, and draw back to a weaker, less desirable position. But compromising can also be seen as skilful diplomacy—the finding of the *via media* (the middle way) and obtaining agreement from disparate, perhaps antagonistic, parties.

To compromise is to trade off one thing for another. So much of business, and personal life, is designing the optimal trade-off of different qualities or values. For all businesses, and also many people, the three most quoted trade-off issues are quality, speed, and cost (see Figure 1.2).

Imagine that you want to commission a piece of work. It may be the manufacturing of a product, a staff survey, the evaluation of a management process, or the purchase of a new IT system. At the most mundane level, you think of getting in an artisan (plumber, painter, decorator) to work on your house. What you want is for the work to be good, fast, and cheap. Naturally, you want the quality of the work to be high; you want the work done quickly so as to minimize the disruption to the house; and you certainly want the work to be cheap (affordable, value for money).

FIGURE 1.2 THE TRADE-OFF
DILEMMA IN ALL BUSINESS

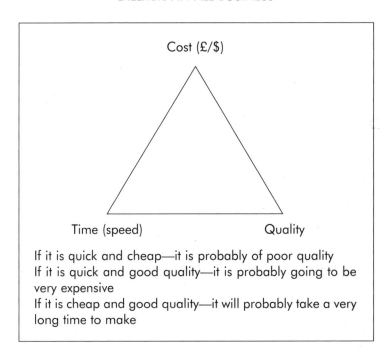

Cost (£/$)

Time (speed)   Quality

If it is quick and cheap—it is probably of poor quality
If it is quick and good quality—it is probably going to be
very expensive
If it is cheap and good quality—it will probably take a very
long time to make

Alas, trading off means not getting the maximum amount of all three, but trading off one against another. You can usually have two of the three, but not all three together. Consider the organizations and managers who typically trade off one of the three.

Good and cheap, but not fast

This is where speed is traded off for quality and price. In this sense, quality can be cost-effective, but at the price of speed. If you are prepared to wait for people to work at their own speed, or when their erratic timetable allows, they may do the job well (even relatively cheaply), but it does drag on. Amateurs, part-timers, and enthusiasts often perform tasks with total commitment and with relatively little reward, but they cannot be rushed.

Some organizations believe that quality is worth the wait. They may even argue that there is no alternative (the thing cannot be rushed), or indeed, that time spent is an index of quality. Research and development scientists, academics, writers, and so on believe that they can come up with the goods only if they are not hurried. The "folksy" family restaurant may provide uncommonly good food at very affordable prices—but at its own speed.

Individuals differ in their time sense and their impulsivity. The time-poor, cash-rich certainly would not make this trade-off.

Good and fast, but not cheap

This is where price is traded off for speed and quality. If you want high-quality work with a very short lead time, you must be prepared to pay for it. In a sense, this is the concept of overtime. You can get sophisticated professionals (lawyers, doctors, engineers) to work through the night to provide excellent results, but you need to be prepared to pay for it. High flyers working to a tight delivery date command high salaries. There is always a cost, which is money.

Some businesses are used to frenetic output. They believe things have to be "right first time" and on time—and they are prepared to pay for it. Looking back, it seems incredible to see what the rush was all about, but at the time, no one seems to question it. Money can buy hard work, commitment, and quality.

This is the "you get what you pay for" mentality. People, it seems, are prepared to work long hours on highly complex projects, but they will want to be fairly (read equitable or highly) compensated for their endeavor.

Fast and cheap, but not good

This is where quality is traded off for speed and price. This is the cheap and cheerful, "pile 'em high and sell 'em cheap" end of the market. The fast-food industry does not pretend to offer fine dining. It provides cheap and tasty (semi, quasi, crypto) nutritious food served immediately. Naturally, organizations and individuals that trade off this way do not neglect quality; they merely set a lower standard.

You can buy products and hire people at highly competitive prices, but most people rightly suspect that just as there is no such thing as a free lunch, there are very rarely any real bargains. In the end, you get what you pay for. And if it is really cheap and quickly done, it is rarely very good.

Some people (read bargain hunters) are suspicious of the "link" between quality and price. They believe that things can be produced fast and cheaply, and that quality will suffice.

Consider the 12 choices in Table 1.1 for yourself, and how you think a colleague would respond. They all involve trade-offs: time versus money, education versus cash, space versus cash, and so on. What does this say about you and your preferences? More importantly, does it suggest that you believe you are similar to, or different from, others?

Your boss calls you in and makes you an offer. For reasons too problematic to explain, you have the following option: a week's extra leave (five working days) or £2,000 cash (brown envelope, no questions asked!). You choose the week, so your boss increases the money. How about £2,500? So if you take the money, your boss increases the time: eight days.

This very simple choice can prove surprisingly diagnostic. At the crudest level it tells you how much people are paid. Go around a room full of executives playing the game and you can get a very good indicator of "who's who." Sometimes senior people will hold out for over £5,000 for a week's extra holiday. That's £1,000 a day, but it seems to have little impact on them. Others will take as little as £750, presumably because they need the money or love their job.

Cash rich, time poor (CRTP) is associated with age and stage. Middle-aged people have more money but feel they need more time. People who work in the public sector

TABLE 1.1 TWELVE TRADE-OFFS

	Your choice	What would a colleague choose?	Report
1. £1,500 cash or a week off work	___	___	___
2. Top business school course worth £8,000 or £2,500 cash	___	___	___
3. Free holiday for four people in the Caribbean or £2,000 cash	___	___	___
4. £500 or double your office space	___	___	___
5. £1,000 shares or £800 cash	___	___	___
6. The next promotion you apply for, but only half your current salary rate increase	___	___	___
7. Nominated manager of the year or £100 M&S vouchers	___	___	___
8. Free tickets to the opera/ sport (value £400) or two long weekends	___	___	___
9. A company car or free BUPA	___	___	___
10. British Airways vouchers worth £3,000 or two weeks off work	___	___	___
11. Guaranteed parking space or free canteen food	___	___	___
12. Top-up pension opportunities or one week increase in your annual leave	___	___	___

often need more money than those in the private sector. US workers, who may have only two weeks' holiday a year, certainly are time poor.

What does being CRTP do to people? The well-paid executive (say, north of £250,000), the shareholder-pressured CEO, the industrious management consultant; all have lots of demands on their time. So much so, they often experience price insensitivity. This may apply to big and small things.

Shopping, at least for men, is more likely to be a chore than a pleasure. CRTP executives often whiz around stores simply putting in the shopping basket things that they fancy, need, or think they need. They do not bother about the price or brand comparisons to maximize value. Further, they may choose things that seem preposterously overpriced simply to save time. They might be price insensitive, but are easily sold on time-saving products.

CRTP managers are fans of GAMI not DIY. "Get a man in" is the response to both household and managerial problems. Do-it-yourself is a foreign concept. They are prepared to call in anybody who can help—now, and they mean *now*! And this has led to the re-emergence of (effectively) servants. Of course they are not called that any more, but there is a new class of servants who job it is to give CRTP managers more time. These personal assistants may do everything from walking the dog to serving food at dinner parties or even negotiating property deals. Their jobs are, in effect, to liberate CRTP people from the chores they do not enjoy.

The CRTP dilemma has also generated a new concept: quality time. This is usually referred to as the time tired and listless executives spend with their children. The wonder and joy of a five year old wears off surprisingly quickly, so time-sensitive CRTP managers are often tempted to read the paper, watch the television, or simply doze off soon after seeing their children or their spouse.

Quality time means being fully engaged, attentive, disclosive, empathetic, and the rest. It's hard if you are all "peopled out" and simply want to relax with a glass of claret and the paper. It is not uncommon for CRTP managers to have marital problems: their spouses feel neglected, even spurned; their children are rebellious and taciturn; even their servants may express job dissatisfaction.

It is tough at the top: the rewards are high, but so are the costs. Time is indeed money. The question of course is whether the fame is worth the effort. Remember, few people on their deathbed ever said they wished they had spent more time at work.

The issue here is what people will sacrifice for money; what they are prepared to trade off for the acquisition and accumulation of money. It is said that everybody has his or her price. In this sense it means that people would do dirty, dangerous, or demeaning work for money at the right level. People will trade off job security for salary, even job title for salary. Much depends on their age and stage, how much money they have accumulated or believe they can accumulate; their personality and preferences, motives, and morals. And, of course, it depends on what they *really* want the money for.

All money is acquisition and about trade-off. Indeed we call it compensation (Comp & Ben) no doubt because we believe it somehow compensates for doing something no one else really wants to do.

INTRINSIC AND EXTRINSIC MOTIVATION

It is extremely important to understand and differentiate between intrinsic and extrinsic motivation. Intrinsic means belonging to the essential nature of the activity. It is about something that originates within something. It is part of its very nature of being. The antonym is extrinsic: it means originating from the outside. It's extraneous.

We are, and can be, motivated both intrinsically and extrinsically. We are intrinsically motivated to do things we love doing. We are extrinsically motivated by money to do things we find less appealing, possibly stressful, frequently boring.

Intrinsically motivating jobs require somewhat less compensation and benefit than extrinsically motivating jobs. But what is the difference? It can be illustrated by the following true story.

A university lecturer was scribbling at home. Things were going well. But because it was a public holiday, the local park was full of children laughing and playing. Their erratic, loud, uncontrollable noise was deeply disturbing. And there was no easy alternative for the lecturer. Closing the windows did little to muffle the sound, only making the room stuffy. There was no other room to decamp to. So what was there to do, other than, as they say, "move the children on"?

Possibilities arise: threaten the children or bribe them to go away. The method is well known to the mafia. The children might accept the bribe but soon return to this lucrative source of money.

The academic, however, knew his motivation theory. He wandered out, to confront the noisy interference. Mustering all the charm he could, he gathered the children around him and told them that he had observed them from his office and had admired and enjoyed their noisy games, high-spirited yells and laughter so much that he was prepared to pay them to continue. Each child was given a pound.

Of course they continued. The wise lecturer did the same the next day and the next. But on the fourth day he sallied forth and the expectant children gathered around. He explained that for various reasons he had no money so he could no longer continue to "subsidize" the play. Speaking on behalf of the others, the oldest child said that if he thought the children were going to carry on playing for nothing he was sadly misinformed, and they "were off, never to return."

What the lecturer knew was that the essence of play is that it is intrinsically satisfying. It is a preposterous idea to pay people to play, because they love and volunteer for the activity. You only have to recompense people for doing things they *do not* really enjoy: things that are dangerous or mind-numbingly dreary; things that are tiring or stressful.

In 1990 a psychologist, Milay Csikszentmihalyi, wrote a book called *Flow* that tried to describe and explain the magical state of pleasure that people get from doing their favorite activity. This maybe hiking, or hang-gliding; singing *the Messiah* in a full choir, or carefully tending to a loved garden. They are, for enthusiasts, deeply satisfying experiences; engrossing and enriching; beguiling and very personally rewarding.

Hobbies and pastimes are very varied, and quite clearly one person's meat is another's poison. A day at an allotment, an evening fishing by the canal, or a morning on the virgin piste is heaven for some and hell for others. So is flow a deeply individual experience? There are jobs that may offer many flow opportunities and others practically none at all. Consider some really rotten jobs, such as a traffic warden, or a security guard—unbelievably tedious, occasionally dangerous—or working on a dreary production line in a noisy, dirty factory.

Two indicators of pay level are first, how long it takes to master the skill and knowledge to do the job, and second, the responsibilities that go with it.

Naturally there comes a point in all deeply intrinsically motivating jobs where people make the choice between lifestyles. People in the City (London's financial district) are conspicuously extrinsically motivated. They want high earnings before retirement at 40 (or 50). They are prepared to put up with very long hours of stressful work for lots of money if it allows them to do something intrinsically motivating afterwards.

The really hard question is how to motivate those whose job is not, and probably cannot be, intrinsically motivating. How do you motivate people gutting chickens in a cold factory on a deprived estate?

There are no easy answers, but there are things that can be done. These workers often want a sense of belonging and autonomy. So they form self-managed teams. Give them clear goals and guidelines and a lot of help to begin with; but let them decide how they achieve their goals and they do become interested, particularly if there are rewards attached to performance.

You can never make extrinsically motivating jobs as attractive as those with very clear intrinsic features, but something can be done.

But, as we shall see, there can be a real danger in using money as a main reward (where that is possible) It can have paradoxical effects of demotivating workers, because their focus now moves to what is intrinsically attractive about the job, to what they get compensation for.

BOOK THEMES

This book is essentially divided into three sections, which are related and overlapping. Chapter 2 looks at money at work. It focuses on the classic, complex and controversial question concerning the motivational role of money at work. The answer to the question is fundamentally important for anyone managing a business. It looks at the theory but also gives some practical advice.

Chapters 3 and 4 look at the individual, and the origins and manifestations of normal and abnormal money beliefs. The two chapters look at money messages we get from childhood and the many types of money-troubled people there are, and consider why educated and informed people don't think straight about money.

Chapter 5 looks at wider aspects of money in society, and makes the link between money and religion and political development. It also looks at the relationship between money and happiness.

Here are some observations from our reading and personal experience:

1. People who are happy about their money (income, wages, investments) are happy about other aspects of their life. This is not because money leads to happiness, but there tend to be happy people and unhappy people. Life satisfaction, job satisfaction, and pay satisfaction are closely linked. There is not therefore

a major impact on happiness by adding or subtracting money.

2. Pay is *one* of the rewards at work. There are others both tangible and intangible. It is difficult to separate these, as many are inextricably linked. People think about their total percentage. They make trade-offs. At certain times of their life, and because of their base-rate pay, money may take on a very important role. But it is way down the list in predicting why people choose jobs and the satisfaction they have in them.

3. Money is a motivator in how people choose jobs and how they work in them. But its power is particularly limited if: people consider themselves amply or satisfactorily paid; they are not very materialistic; they feel fairly paid compared both to others and their self experience. In those cases it remains relatively stable. By contrast, money works as a motivator where people can perform for it; they believe they need it; it is truly related to performance; they find the work highly pleasurable and intrinsically rewarding.

4. The power of money to demotivate is higher than its power to motivate. It is more a source of anxiety and envy than a source of pleasure. People see money as a demotivator if they feel they are not fairly paid compared with others. Money is an easy, powerful social comparator. It is a way of measuring.

5. People do not behave as logical, rational individuals as economists assume. Even without money pathology they make well-known and systematic "errors" in how they use money. The symbolic power of money stops them being rational. These odd money-related decisions are well known and documented. Knowing about them helps us make better money decisions.

6. Attitudes and beliefs about the use of money are closely tied up with other beliefs, because both its symbolic and actual value. Further, formal and informal money education begins early. It has been claimed that the signs of early entrepreneurship can be seen in the school playground. Millionaires are made, not born. We can and should teach young people to be better managers of their own money. Money education is, or should be, the concern of *every* parent and teacher.

7. Money attitudes are tied to other political, religious, and economic beliefs. In this sense money is an ideological issue. The distributions and correlations of wealth are at the heart of politics. The use and abuse of money are at the heart of religion. Thus all aspects of money usage from charity giving to tax evasion are linked.

8. There are a surprising number of money-troubled people. These are people whose beliefs about money lead them to behaving in ways that can cause and perpetuate unhappiness. Because of the symbolic value of money as a source of security, love, power, and freedom, people can hurt themselves and others by their irrational psychological rather than logical behavior.

9. As society changes, so do our attitudes to money. People think about money quite differently in poor or rich countries, in high or low-tax countries, and in countries with high and low inflation. Governments can and do punish and reward certain money behaviors (especially saving) with mixed success. They too make trade-offs.

10. Motivation is a hard topic for various reasons. One is that people *cannot*, rather than *will not*, tell you about

what really motivates them. Regardless of to what extent they believe in the power of the murky unconscious, what is clearly evident is that people often do not understand what motivates them to do such strange things with their money. Therapists spend a lot of time helping people become aware of the deep springs of their motivation. And this does not just apply to the seriously disturbed patient. Understanding and articulating our own motives often seems harder then understanding those of others.

Money is a poor motivator for four reasons:

- *Adaptation*: The effects of increases in money, salary, or reward very soon wear off.
- *Comparison*: It is not the absolute amount of money you earn/receive that is motivating but how much it is relative to your immediate social comparison group.
- *Alternatives*: What you have to give up for the pursuit of money (time, security, on so on).
- *Worry*: About envy, tax, burglary, and so on.

Pay someone inequitably and you have a *very* demotivated individual. Pay them equitably, but you still need to do many more things at work to achieve a contented and productive individual.

2

Money and motivation

Getting money is like digging with a needle; spending it is like water soaking into sand.

(Japanese Proverb)

INTRODUCTION

Money is a means to a life, a status symbol, a reason for respect and jealousy, but above all, it is seen as a work motivator. It is said that "If you pay peanuts you get monkeys." But is the opposite true: "If you pay gold bars you will get Stakhanovites"? The ability of money to motivate a work force to greater performance and productivity has been an important issue, and central to much economic theory, for many years.

Much work in economics draws on what has been termed the "relative price effect." It maintains that an individual's motivation to complete a task increases when the reward or price rises in comparison with the reward or price of the current market alternatives. So the more that a worker is offered, above what he or she can receive from another source, the more likely the worker is to be motivated to complete the said task. Therefore, one may conclude that individuals are encouraged to work harder as their financial incentive becomes greater. This effect can be easily seen in nearly all day-to-day transactions. It is no surprise that the best paid jobs, in the best companies, attract the greatest competition among workers, or that in the January sales you see queues of hundreds of people clambering to get into the big department stores such as Selfridges, all to gain that elusive bargain.

The motivational effects of money or reward on productivity and performance are far from simple. A rise

FIGURE 2.1 REWARD/PRODUCTIVITY POSSIBLE OUTCOMES

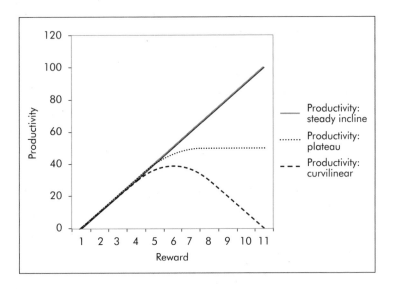

in reward can cause change to the performance or productivity of any given individual, in a number of ways.

Figure 2.1 shows three possible effects that a steady increase in reward may have on the productivity of the worker. First, *steady linear incline* suggests that there is a linear relationship between reward and productivity. Here quite simply, as the size of the reward (money) increases, so too does the level of productivity of the worker—more money means more motivation and more output, and more happiness. The linear relationship poses one significant problem, in that there may be a peak to which human productivity can reach, and perhaps more importantly, also a peak reward that the business world would be willing and able to offer. But can an individual's physical capability to produce, no matter the reward or desire of the worker to reach that target, meet the expectation of the employer? Second, is the employer ready and willing to make continuing incremental increases to induce the increased productivity required?

A second possibility is that productivity will *plateau.* Here productivity will increase in linear fashion with reward up to a certain point. At this point the influence of other environmental factors, such as work environment, job role, family and friends, or management will take effect, and subsequent increase in reward will balance out these other variables, leading productivity to plateau. There is also a point where the ability of business to continually increase the reward given to its employees will cease to be cost-effective. When reward increase is stopped, then again we may expect a plateau in productivity. This refers back to the trade-off concept. Here money has an effect up to a point. It is another form of the 80:20 rule known as Pareto's principle. An Italian economist, Pareto, observed that 20 percent of the population (this was in Italy around 1900) owned 80 percent of the wealth. There are now many adaptations of this rule. Thus 20 percent of your work consumes 80 percent of your time and resources. Or an 80 percent increase in effort will only result in a 20 percent increase in productivity, then 90 percent and 10 percent, and finally 100 percent and nothing.

The third possibility, *rise and fall (curvilinear),* suggests that at the point at which the other variables begin to affect the reward–productivity relationship, rather than forming a plateau, productivity begins to decrease. More becomes less. Paradoxically the incentive of large sums of money has this negative effect on productivity. People become fat and lazy, contented and overfed, overpaid and complacent.

A fourth and final possibility is that there will be *no relationship*. It is possible that some individuals simply are not motivated by money to any extent. This is certainly true of many religious groups from all cultures, Buddhist, Christian, and Hindu, who reject materialism for spiritualism. They have the philosophy of "to be" rather than "to have." Equally there are those who are quite content to do what they like doing, are good at it, or believe it to be important irrespective of the financial reward.

There are other patterns of course. Show Figure 2.1 to people. Explain the options, and see what they think. Nobody believes in options one and four, a steady linear effect and no relationship. Of course reward (money) influences effort (productivity). The question is how that relationship works.

THE MEANING OF MONEY

What money means to each individual affects greatly how money will influence his or her day-to-day living. Certainly people from Western societies protect information on their financial situation with greater vigor than they do information on their sex lives. Many people find information on their financial situations more embarrassing, or more harmful to their self-esteem, self-confidence, and so on, than information on their sex lives.

Money's intimate nature is not the same as sex, in that it is physical; it has form. Its privacy comes from its influence on our lives. Money is a source of social acceptance. It limits or allows for things we can and cannot have, and because of this, it is tied to our beliefs about ourselves, our confidence, and our self-esteem. For no group of people is this inexplicable tie of finance and money to self and worth more apparent than for philosophic materialists. The high-level materialist values possessions, and the esteem and pride taken from ownership of commodities. Money allows these individuals to buy such commodities when, where, and in what volumes they require.

Much has been written about materialism and post-materialism. By definition post-materialists are less interested in money, but there are those who pretend.

Materialist

These people can be unfairly and crudely stereotyped. Greed is good. Those who have most toys win—it's survival of the richest. They are *homo economicus*, relatively simple organisms designed to increase their happiness by wealth accumulation, which is believed to be good for all. They are logical, rational, and objective at work. They are readily incentivized by money, status, security, and the like. Work is a price people pay for money. Money brings freedom, choice, love, power, security, and respect. Managers and employees know where they stand.

Post-materialist

These people either may not or cannot be managed, because they don't work for big profit organizations. They are into self-expression, creativity and harmony. They work out their own value systems and have little time for all those triumphs of the enlightenment, such as democracy and the big institutions of law, education, and business.

Post-materialist people always emphasize quality over quantity, being over having, subjectivity over objectivity.

They may happily "work" together in communities, collectives, and consortia, but can be surprisingly dictatorial about non-dictatorial behavior.

Hence money's value is not embedded in them as a physical thing, but in what it can be exchanged for, and the improved sense of self and improved social standing that this represents. It is easy to imagine the admiration and jealousy among friends (admittedly more likely male friends) that the man who appears one day in a brand new Aston Martin might command.

And with money's power to elevate status, it also has the power to cause a metamorphosis of people, from what they are today, to what they aspire to be. Here the meaning of money is its transformational, mystical power, its ability to make the impossible reality, to make what were once dreams into an everyday event.

Money also means freedom. Money is seen as freedom to buy want you want, when you want, from whom you want, and under whichever conditions you want. But more than this, money means an extensive freedom of experience. In an economy driven by consumption, experience is given a value, and unless you have money equal to this value, the experience is out of reach. This is perhaps one of the clearest examples of how the meaning of money affects our motivation to be productive and gain reward.

It is somewhat paradoxical that in order to gain the freedom of experience that money allows us, we have to a certain extent given up our everyday freedom to do what we want and work, as if we do not work, we do not gain a salary. There is a certain irony, albeit unavoidable in a Western economic culture, that we have to buy our freedom of experience with money gained through the sale of our everyday freedom.

The mystical money transformation

We are all familiar with the story of Cinderella, the poor, beautiful young woman, tied to a life of slavery by her evil stepsisters. One day her fairy godmother arrives to whisk her away into the arms of a handsome prince, who will rid her of her life of drudgery, and elevate her to new status and into a world of opportunity.

Now does this classic fairy tale sound any different from the modern concept of the sugar daddy and the dolly girl? Surely the young ladies who hanker for a rich husband really desire the same things as Cinderella: The chance to better oneself through the acquisition of a man with money who can offer more than her current situation. For this is surely what the Prince is offering to Cinderella. The fact that he is always described as the handsome Prince, or Prince Charming, could be seen as either a validation of Cinderella's desire, or as an encapsulation of the positive effects of money.

Perhaps this is rather a skeptical view of a classical fairytale, but in both scenarios the assumption is that money has this mystical power to generate not only a greater ability to consume, to own, but it will also empower the individual to improve as a person: To take the examples from the Cinderella story, to grow stronger, less fearful, more charming, wiser, less vulnerable, and so on. It is this notion of the transformational powers of money towards human betterment that so inspires many to seek it with such vigor and deliberateness.

Money also holds a sacred meaning, not simply for those who have such a desire to gain more and more wealth that they worship money, but in the sense that it is ritualized. There has been some suggestion by researchers that religious-based rituals such as funerals and weddings amass such great cost not out of love for those who have passed on, but instead, there is a belief that in some way the money spent buys a passage to heaven, or to a happy life, and in this process it sacralizes the occasion. This would appear to be the ultimate application of the "everything and everyone has their price" mentality, perhaps suggesting that the doors to heaven themselves have a price tag attached. And let us not forget of course, the Protestant ethic is based on the idea that accumulation, but not consumption of wealth, displays to God the leading of a virtuous and hard-working life.

Lea and Webley (1999) have suggested two reasons for our pursuit of money. First, money is a tool: not a weapon but an instrument. Money is not an incentive in itself, but because it can be exchanged for goods and services. We live in a token economy, and what we carry in our pockets are tokens and nothing more. The value of paper money or coins is not intrinsic. The paper and the metal are worth a pittance. The need and desire we have for them stem from their exchangeable value.

A good example of how the token economy works is the theme park. On entry we exchange money for wristbands or tickets. These are the currency of exchange once we are within the walls of the park. They can be exchanged for "goes" on each ride, on games stools, and in some cases for food and drink to a certain value. The bands and tickets are worthless, but by their acquisition, we get to experience all the theme park has to offer. The only way the outside world's economy differs from this theme park token economy is that our tokens need to provide us with more than just experience, though the principles are the same.

The second reason for our possible attraction to money is of far more interest. *Drug theory* states that we have an addiction to money, in a similar way as we become addicted to alcohol, nicotine, or heroin. Money is a "perceptual drug." It does not act by chemical reactions, but on sensory reactions. Money's motivational power comes from its mimicking of natural incentive, the sensory perception of all the multitude of stimuli, smells, sights, and sounds, and so on that influence cognitive processing.

In essence there is no logical reason why we would continually desire money, beyond our own subsistence, in much the same way as there is no logic behind a continued desire to smoke cigarettes or consume alcohol, both of which we know shorten our lives if taken in excess. Yet despite this we consume them, and to varying levels this desire gets very strong, as the desire varies between a social drinker and an alcoholic. If we are exposed to this desire for a greater length of time it can become hazardous to our health and our day-to-day functioning. Again, this is not in the same sense as, say, alcoholism would stop us working, but a desire for money may mean *we do not stop working.* Hence in the former case it is work that is a detriment to the addiction, and in the latter it may be the family, or social contacts, that suffer the wrath of the addiction.

MONEY AS A DEMOTIVATOR

With the greater part of rich people, the chief enjoyment of riches consists in the parade of riches, which in their eye is never so complete as when they appear to possess those decisive marks of opulence which nobody can possess but themselves.

(Smith 1937)

There is no question that money plays a crucial role in our decisions in the workplace and in life as a whole. However, the question here is more specific: Is money a good motivator of work performance?

A recent article by Toynbee (2003) in the British newspaper the *Guardian* highlighted the long list of factors other than pay that now affect workers' satisfaction with their jobs. Although 56 percent of the managers interviewed rated pay as being very important in the decision to stay or leave a job, 54 percent said that enjoyment was also crucial, with 45 percent citing the importance of working hours. In terms of motivation, 59 percent said that they would be encouraged to apply for a job because of the salary, but 50 percent stated that location would be as important. What these statistics highlight is that although money is still a very dominant influence, there are now a wide variety of other variables that affect what some see as being a very direct relationship between money and motivation. Other factors emphasized in the article were relationships with peers and bosses, organizational beliefs—in terms of what the company stands for—quality of work, and chances to enhance skills.

We have been aware for a long time of those jobs where people experience the greatest satisfaction. They are not jobs of power, influence, status, and money, nor are they jobs of selfless giving in the service of others. They are jobs where people have autonomy and the chance to practice their skills. They are craftspeople—potters, painters, thatchers, and writers—often the happiest of all.

One of the major factors in the slow uptake of detailed open research on this topic is that the research has to a large extent been dominated by economics and business:

> Economists, while recognizing that all sorts of non-monetary rewards for performance can be important, tend to focus on monetary rewards because individuals they believe are willing to substitute non-monetary for monetary rewards ...
>
> (Baker, Jenson, and Murphy 1988)

There has also been a prevailing opinion in business for the best part of the last century, that monetary incentive and payment by results is the best way to motivate, and this position has been held despite a lack of empirically researched evidence:

> The manager also consistently expressed the belief that all the workers wanted was money, and that non-financial motives were unimportant.
>
> (Behrend 1988)

This overriding belief that money is still *the* most effective motivator can only prove to be increasingly more problematic to industry and business. Without a fundamental change in the thinking and logic of the business community, and recognition of the powerful but changing factors that are important to its employees, it will be impossible to create and implement affectively motivational schemes of management. It puts those who are trying to alter the thinking of the business community in an awkward position. How well are most executives going to take being told that the logic by which their businesses have been run for as long as they have known them is faulty, inappropriate, and ineffective, and in order to save money and improve the productivity of said business, they need to spend more in realizing what their employees really want? This is not common business logic, and may even be considered counter-intuitive, but this is the reality of the situation.

The earliest studies that suggested the idea that worker performance and productivity could be stimulated by increased pay were those of Taylor, 100 years ago. Taylor's scientific management involved detailed time analysis of a worker, the removal of all unnecessary tasks, and then the offer of a pay system based on results. Taylor's example of the benefits of his system was that of the "thrifty Dutchman." Taylor offered this worker a piece rate pay based on the level of pig iron he could shovel. The Dutchman then upped performance by many hundred percent. On this evidence, and a number of similar studies, Taylor's ideas became the basis of thought for many pay schemes over decades. What Taylor selectively chose not mention in his report of his findings was that his thrifty Dutchman actually died rather early in life for such an evidently strong fit man, and although it was never stated conclusively, many believed he died of exhaustion, or some factor related to his level of work.

Systems such has Taylor's were devised by many other researchers over time. Some systems even went as far as time and motion studies of the most effective and quickest way to take a bath and wash oneself. The notion that workers' performance could be bought by offering wages based on their output has become business logic, and to some extent, traces of this are still evident in business practice today.

If money and financial incentive are to be considered as motivators for work and performance, it must be possible to show that under certain circumstances, where individuals have been offered greater financial incentive, performance has increased significantly. There has been much research showing the significant effect of financial incentive in laboratory, field, and experimental simulation studies. One notable study (Jenkins et al. 1998) has shown the positive effect on performance of incentive. Jenkins and colleagues conducted a large-scale review of research into the effects of money as a motivator between 1975 and 1996. They found that financial incentives had a strong link to performance quantity. Their results went some way to supporting the principles and arguments of expectancy, reinforcement, and goal-setting theories discussed above. They concluded that if money were not an influence, or a motivator, they would have found no consistent findings to suggest an improvement in performance.

Other research evidence has provided findings that cast doubt on money's motivational powers on quality and quantity. But a review undertaken of the work carried out in the 1960s looked at six different studies and concluded there was little evidence to suggest money had any significant motivational influence. Getting people to chase money produces nothing but people chasing money. Observers argued that money's lack of motivational power was not so much down to the money itself, or the pay scheme per se, but instead it lacked the ability to generate motivation because of the mismanagement of pay schemes. Through poor application and understanding at management level, the correct interpretation was not being passed on to the workforce, and hence the desired affect could not be generated.

Again this highlights two points made previously in this section. *First*, an insistence from management that financial incentive will motivate employees will continually cause any new systems to fail or to be disadvantaged, as those implementing them do not believe in, or understand, the basic principles. *Second*, it again emphasizes the importance of the internal communication systems needed to change incentive-based systems.

There is plenty of evidence that pay-for-performance schemes do not work and backfire. There are essentially three reasons for this. *First*, for most jobs it is very difficult to get a robust, comprehensive, and sensitive measurement of the performance of individuals. *Second*, there are very few jobs where pay is tied logically and exclusively to this output quota, because the gap between high and low performers is too high. *Third*, people do not like the internal competitiveness that results from these schemes.

Unions oppose pay for performance. Individuals don't understand it. Managers fudge, particularly when performance amounts to managers' appraisals, which are often seen to be internally biased.

The reason that pay is not a strong motivator is that for many people it lacks salience. If an individual has lots of money, or indeed enough money for his or her needs, either inheritance, winnings, or in particular a high personal salary, then the offer of additional money is not an attractive proposition. It will not stay in the forefront of an employee's mind that if he or she puts in that extra hour each day, or produces another ten items a day, he or she will be given an extra £50, if it only represents a small percentage of what the employee would take home if he or she didn't expend that extra effort. This becomes an extra problem for businesses if we consider the rate at which base salaries are increasing. If the base salary is high, the bonus will also have to be high, and then the cost-effectiveness of the extra effort being asked for becomes questionable.

Work centrality has been used by many researchers to explain the inconsistent evidence of money as a motivational tool. This concept refers to how important work is to our lives, self-image, self-esteem, and how we feel about ourselves. Have you ever been stood at a bar, or worse still had the misfortune of being face to face, with an individual who has nothing to talk about other than work? This is a person whose sole contribution to discussions is another anecdote about a deal he or she sealed, or what policy his or her office had implemented. Although in many cases they are infuriating to talk to, such people would be considered to have very high work centrality. They are their job; their job is them.

It is quite clear from the examples that research on work centrality brought up, that for many workers money is of absolutely no consequence to their motivation to work. Although these examples are extremes, they highlight that money's function as a motivator for work is minimal, and our motivation to get up each morning, put on our uniform (a suit may as well be considered the uniform of the City) and head off for another day at work is much more than the amount of cash in our pockets or the limit on our credit cards. Work, for most, is more than a simple source of income, and any attempt to motivate employees to greater performance must reflect this.

If you want to know what the Lord God thinks of money, you have only to look at those to whom he gives it.

(Maurice Baring, quoted in Dorothy Parker, *Writers at Work: First series*)

If then it is so highly doubtful that money is an effective motivator of performance, why do businesses choose to continue to use such schemes? And why, despite this, why do we as human beings continue to desire money and wealth?

A large part of the work about money as a demotivator has looked at its effect on intrinsic motivation. Rousseau believed any constraints placed on an individual's ability to live, pursue goals, in both the short and long term, and to follow impulse, were not only highly aversive but also infringed on individuals' freedom from social controls. And it is this freedom from social control that underlies human creativity. Any restriction here instantly damages a person's individual creativity and intrinsic motivation. So, does money have this effect?

It has been argued by Deci et al. (1999) that the use of expected financial incentives such as salary, awards, prizes and bonuses, and external motivators, *reduces intrinsic motivation* for the task, and therefore decreases performance. For individuals who are intrinsically motivated, external incentives such as money act as a demotivator for work, as they reward task completion, and pay little attention to the reward gained from the task itself. Intrinsically motivated people will draw their motivation to work from the inherent properties of the task, and the goal of completing it well. Thus, money does not in any way affect the motivation of such people.

Individuals who had been rewarded for tasks were then less inclined to complete tasks that did not have rewards attached to them. This expectancy of reward is important, as it suggests a negative dual effect of financial incentives to work.

When a human being joins a new employer, at some point before the job starts, a wage–work bargain is struck between the employer and employee. This is not a literal contract, but a psychological one. It is never written, but it is understood, that by the acceptance of the job, the worker will generate the expected performance level, and in return the employer will provide good work conditions and a wage. With the wage–work bargain established between worker and employer, there then comes an expectation by the worker for a raise in monetary reward, in return for which he or she increases the volume of work undertaken. These become the outwardly stated criteria, but implicit to this, businesses make the assumption that the quality of the work will also increase, by the same percentage as the quantity. Here, if the explicit statement of the employer is for a 20 percent increase in production, then the implicit requirement is also for a 20 percent rise in quality. In essence the employer is asking for a 40 percent rise in employee performance, under the financial conditions of a 20 percent rise.

In this scenario there are a few things that would be unlikely to happen. The chances of the worker making a natural link between volume and quality are slim. These are not two factors that are causally linked. If there was a rare occurrence of a worker understanding the implicit requirements of the contract, then the disparity and inequity of the deal would become apparent and the targets would not be likely to be fulfilled. The end result of both of these situations would be the removal of the incentive, and perhaps a decrease in pay, and hence decrease in motivation.

There is evidence that under certain circumstances, with an extremely high monetary incentive, people can exert incredible levels of effort to produce both quality and quantity in their work. However, this extraordinary effort must be to the detriment of some other factor. It is then quite possible that there are elements of the job, either work-oriented or social, that do not have solid ties to the receiving of reward, that suffer as a consequence. This may even be represented in people's own utility or that of family and friends.

Some writers really challenge the idea that money increases motivation. Kohn (1993) famously argues that business works on a "Do this and you'll get that" attitude towards motivation and incentive, and that this at best produces some short-term effects on motivation. At worst, it cuts to the fabric of business functioning, and damages far more than could ever be hoped to be gained. Kohn describes five ways in which rewards, specifically financial rewards, damage and demotivate worker motivation and performance:

1. *Rewards punish*: Rewards are a manipulative tool, in the same way as threats. To say "Do this and I will give you this" is as good as saying "Do this or this will happen." This becomes an uncomfortable situation for an employee. A second way in which rewards can punish is through the expectation with no receipt. A promised reward that is not received is psychologically as bad as a punishment, as the increase in positive state is swiftly removed by the disappointment of non-receipt.

2. *Punishments rupture relations*: High performance often requires teamwork. If a group of workers are chasing the same incentive then they will be in a state of competition, and cooperative and really cohesive work will not be possible. The relationship with supervisors is also often damaged. This happens in a number of ways. If supervisors do not give awards if they are not justified, the negative feeling of punishment described above will then damage relations with the supervisor who denied the worker the incentive. Also, workers who are pushing for an incentive will not be inclined to ask for assistance, as they would feel this would be a detriment to their receiving the incentive. As such, there arises a lack of communication between workers and supervisor, as well as between workers themselves.

   This is plainly a major problem for business. There are few situations in the modern business environment where an individual is working alone. Employers seek those who can work well in groups, and rely on group work to generate many of their ideas and policies. If employers are using schemes that ultimately damage the performance of such groups, it may not be rash to say that nearly all of the economy has been falling short of its full potential for many years. Maybe we have never seen a fully functioning team unit.

3. *Rewards ignore reason:* If a company or particular function is not performing, to simply offer a financial incentive to bolster performance ignores the many possible root causes of the problem. This allows financial incentive to be nothing more than a short-term fix, even if it had the capacity to be more. It is in a sense treating the symptom, not the cause, and so

although at the surface all may seem well, the seeds and roots of the problem will still lie beneath.

4. *Rewards deter risk taking*: When there is money at stake, individuals are far more likely to take the easy tried and tested option. This conservatism then removes all elements of risk taking, exploration of possibilities, and a desire to follow a hunch or take any action that is not directly related to the task for which the incentive was assigned. This favoring of the easy, simple, and straightforward tasks in the face of incentive has been proven in a wealth of research studies.

5. *Rewards undermine interest*: The enjoyment of a task is a far more powerful influence than any incentive can be. As human beings we carry out far too many tasks that use a large majority of our time but for which we don't receive any other incentive than enjoyment. Hobbies, charity work, and even raising a family all fall into this category. Kohn emphasizes that the more the financial incentive is pushed into the faces of workers, the more this will become their only reason for continuing the task. Therefore if at any point the incentive is no longer one that is desired, then the workers will have no reason to continue the task; their motivation will have gone.

Consider Lent. Many of us try, or have tried, to give up something for Lent. Lent becomes a good time for us to do this as, aside from its religious meaning, it provides a target period of 40 days and 40 nights to begin our abstinence. Now how many of us who have intended to, say, permanently reduce alcohol intake to one night a week, or give up chocolate, and have used Lent as a starting point, have actually continued beyond Lent? The process

Kohn highlights is at work here too. During Lent, especially the first week, we are continually asked what we have given up. In the face of this, despite our intentions to give up something completely, and simply use Lent as a starting point, our focus shifts. We begin to associate the giving up of alcohol, or chocolate, or whatever it may be, to Lent. Then, if we have made it that far, when the 40 days and nights are over, our reason for our abstinence has been removed, our motivation decreases, and we return to our usual alcohol-swilling, chocolate-scoffing ways. Financial incentive for Kohn plays the same role as Lent in our example. It takes the attention away from the real reason for our actions, and on its removal or ending we lose the only reason for the task that we had, and so our motivation for it decreases.

To draw an analogy from Kohn's work, this comes back nicely to the theory of money as a drug: Companies switching between merit-pay schemes are akin to an alcoholic switching from vodka to gin. It is the same effect, only from a new poison. The ultimate irony of the situation is that many would argue that a fundamental change in the reward and management system would cost far too much to implement, and so is not viable. But when we consider the fees paid out in order to develop a new variation of the old faulty system, and the potential productivity benefits of changing to a more highly motivational and functional one, then surely we see it is the current practice that should be abandoned as not being financially viable.

With such a negative opinion on the effect of the merit-pay schemes devised by consultants to motivate workers, Kohn proposes a simple three-rule method to produce motivated workers:

1. Pay people well.
2. Pay people fairly.
3. Then do everything possible to take money off people's minds.

Simplicity itself. Do you think you, or your boss, would feel satisfied if your company had paid Kohn to consult and these were the only three points of advice he gave? Probably not. But the reality is that these small pieces of advice carry more value than a 50-page document piled high with buzz words and business jargon which proposes "radical overhauls" in favor of a "revolutionary new system" that is in fact no different in its basic principles from the one it is replacing.

One group of researchers has endeavored to refute these ideas (Eisenberger, Rhoades, and Cameron 1999). They have suggested that financial incentive, far from decreasing autonomy, actually leads to an increase. This is because through the offering of rewards, the individual giving the reward puts across a message of lack of control over those who receive it. Thus recipients have the option whether to accept the offer of reward or not. Hence autonomy is maintained. Workers then feel more content and happy with their situation, believing they have autonomy and control over their work environment, and so will be happier and more motivated in their work.

Various other researchers have also found counter-evidence to the findings that reward decreases intrinsic motivation and task interest. It has been shown that performance-contingent reward increases intrinsic motivation by making people care about doing a task well, and that there is a positive relationship between expectant reward for high performance and interest in job activities.

One key factor that has been bought to light by the wealth of research into reward and motivation is the idea of *specificity*. The content of tasks and the context in which they are presented, including reward, increase intrinsic motivation when it is conveyed that the task performance helps satisfy needs, wants, or desires. The opposite effect of this is that when the content and context communicate that a task is unimportant, irrelevant, or uninteresting, intrinsic motivation will be decreased. Hence if the task has an obvious tie to an important outcome, and its value is clearly evident to those completing the task, any reward attached to the task will increase intrinsic motivation.

This highlights the importance of having specific and visible goals attached to rewards, and would suggest that rewards should only be imparted when the task has a clear importance, and not simply for day-to-day tasks. Reward for trivial tasks creates the impression that a task is unimportant and inconsequential, and thus motivation to complete the task decreases. It is possible to see how this may cast doubt on the effect that annual bonuses have on staff. Many companies give an annual yearly bonus that is not tied to performance. We may well be led to the conclusion that as the context and content of task throughout the year have no link to the annual bonus, the annual bonus itself offers no incentive for staff on a day-to-day basis to strive for improved performance.

The debate about the effect money incentives have on motivation is sure to continue for many years. Do they increase both internal and external motivation and hence productivity? Do they damage both? Can they work as a short-term solution, but not as a long-term solution? Currently these questions cannot be answered assuredly, with proven sound theory and research. What we can say with a great deal of assurance is that there are many other variables that affect the relationship of money and motivation. Motivation is a human mental state, and as such is susceptible to the influence of a variety of other similar states. The following sections discuss the effects of and relationships between happiness, personality, attitude, and emotion on motivation and productivity.

PSYCHOLOGICAL THEORIES OF MOTIVATION

Perhaps the best known of all money theories is Maslow's. Certainly it is the one that is still taught on all management courses around the world. It is one of the simplest.

Maslow's hierarchy of needs (Figure 2.2) maintained that human beings are influenced by a variety of needs, arranged in a hierarchy. When a person fulfils one of the lower-order needs, he or she immediately focuses on achieving the next level of need. The ultimate goal of any individual is to reach the top of Maslow's hierarchy and achieve "self-actualization." Self-actualization occurs when an individual has developed to the extent that he or she has reached his or her full potential. This is a slightly troublesome concept. We think for most people it is almost impossible for them to imagine ever reaching their full potential.

Maslow's structure of needs did not make specific reference to the influence of, or need for, money. What is obvious is that money is certainly not a higher-order need, concerned with self-esteem, recognition, and attention from others, in order to self-actualize. Money

FIGURE 2.2 MASLOW'S HIERARCHY OF NEEDS

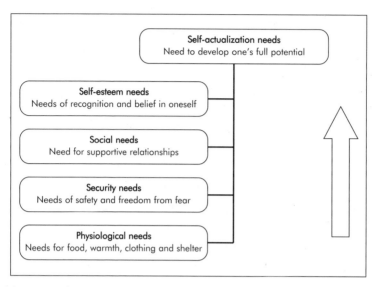

Source: Maslow (1954)

would allow the fulfillment of predominantly lower-order needs. It allows us to eat, drink, and have shelter and clothes. It also to some extent secures our safety needs. In general, it allows us a secure home and perhaps the opportunity to live in a nice area. It pays taxes that provide us with the police, fire services, the army, and hospitals. It may even loosely provide some of our social needs. It allows us free time to pursue various activities or hobbies which offer us the chance to socialize with others of similar interest. However, money is not necessary for us to have social interaction, it only facilitates it, and it is here that money's potential as a motivator stops within Maslow's model. Maslow's higher-order needs are concerned with the endeavor of bettering human potential and the self; they are about emotional and psychological improvement. Money, therefore, is not of great importance in Maslow's formation of human motivation.

The second most well-known theory is Herzberg's motivational-hygiene (two-factor) theory. It postulates that there are two groups of influences that affect motivation. The first are *motivators*, which involve achievement, advancement, recognition, and autonomy. Motivators represent sources of satisfaction for workers. The second group of influences was named *hygiene* factors, and includes supervision, salary, work environment, company policy, and relationships with colleagues. These represent a possible source of dissatisfaction. The presence of motivators improves performance and generates a motivated and satisfied workforce. However their absence does not cause dissatisfaction. Hygiene factors, when present, create an acceptable work environment without increasing individual dissatisfaction. What it is important to note however, is that the absence of hygiene factors causes job dissatisfaction. Salary for Herzberg was a hygiene factor. Thus the need for money was a necessary condition in order to avoid dissatisfaction. It was not sufficient to generate job satisfaction and motivation in the workforce. Money then is a motivator. Get it right and it stops dissatisfaction. However, it has the power more to frustrate than motivate.

The theory suggests that if people are fairly, equitably paid in line with market forces, their skills, and loyalty, they will not become dissatisfied. Even if they are particularly generously paid, they will not experience a greater level of satisfaction or motivation: They will simply be happy in their situation. If however, they are not equitably paid, they will become dissatisfied and presumably unproductive. *This money (salary, wages, income) has the power only to fend off negative feelings, not encourage positive ones.* Money here is only a potential demotivator, not a potential motivator.

The real importance of these theories, both dating back 50 years, is not the content per se, but that they were the first sign of a real change in thinking, suggesting that money may not be the strongest motivator of human performance. In short, we are not all mercenary creatures striving for extra earnings to improve ourselves. Since this time, a plethora of psychological theories have been applied to the debate of money as a motivator of work and performance. Though it is beyond the scope of this current book to discuss every theory in depth, some discussion is necessary. What follows are the basic beliefs of a number of the more widely researched theories within psychology.

> Money, it turned out, was exactly like sex, you thought of nothing else if you didn't have it and thought of other things if you did.
>
> (James A. Baldwin, American novelist and essayist)

HOW DO YOU MOTIVATE PEOPLE AT WORK?

There are some well-known straightforward and all-important ways to motivate staff:

1. *Pay people what they are worth.* Consider market forces, predatory competitors, as well as individual contribution. Consider what insurers call replacement costs. Most people benchmark their salary more regularly than do their employers. Feeling inequitably

paid—that is, paid less than the market rate—is sure to make people very unhappy and demotivated.

2. *Pay attention to individual differences and personal needs.* Ask each employee what motivates him or her, and consider a menu of well-calibrated reward to choose from. Consider employees' free-time activities, and create opportunities for them to use these skills in their activities at work. Just as we have flextime to suit individual preferences, consider other aspects of free choice. The work–life balance issues and flextime are very important.

3. *Give all employees work that is as meaningful as possible.* The less intrinsically interesting the work, the more motivational is anything that is done to encourage job enrichment. This often means job rotations, job sharing, or job enriching. To enrich jobs may make employees less efficient—but more happy. This is a seriously important trade-off that is worth considering.

4. *Give employees the information they need to do a good job.* Make sure they know their priorities, and give them the appropriate tools and training for the job. For some, this can be expressed in jargon of setting key objectives, or key result areas.

5. *Select your people with an eye to motivation.* There are unhappy people who are unhappy and demotivated everywhere, at home and at work. They are carriers of gloomy despondency. They often do not even respond to generous amounts of money. Try to identify them and remove them from the organization.

6. *Train and reward managers for good management.* Help managers to understand the nature of the management role and how to motivate staff. Select for cognitive ability and emotional intelligence. Teach them the skills

of leadership and management, and reward them for doing it well with praise, promotion, and pay.

7. *Make sure wage differentials within the company accurately reflect levels of skill, responsibility, and importance.* Salary needs to be a function of many things, including service and organizational change. Reward, including pay, must be tied to experience, knowledge, and so on.

8. *Keep salaries confidential.* Discourage pay comparisons, though it may be inevitable, by not openly publishing pay levels or individual salaries. The problem is that observers do not always fully understand the nature of the job; they focus too much on observable outputs like pay and benefits.

9. *Offer employees a share of profits.* Let them feel part of the organization as being one of many stakeholders. There are ways to ensure that employees feel part of the family—all on the same side—but these are rarely done at a lower level.

10. *Demonstrate as much as possible a commitment to long-term employment, career development, and promotion from within.* Do not always assume the best talent is outside the organization. Grow your staff.

11. *Reward commitment.* This is demonstrated by loyalty and continuous performance. Most companies now do the opposite, punishing loyalty. It is deeply alienating to believe that no one, apart from yourself, is doing anything about your career.

12. *Provide regular specific feedback to all staff.* Make sure they all know what their bosses (and customers) feel and want. Ask the average employee when he or she last had 30 minutes with the boss discussing just performance issues. Few will say this has happened in

the past five years. Giving progress reviews is cheap, easy, important, and motivating.

13. *Publicly recognize and personally congratulate employees regularly for good work and, more specifically, after good work occurs.* Celebrate success—create heroes. Many British companies find the idea faintly embarrassing, or are scared that they may create jealousy. Public signs of appreciation are as powerful as they are cheap.

14. *Foster a sense of community or teamwork.* Include recognition as part of morale-building meetings that celebrate group success. Make it apparent that most people at work are interdependent. Provide sufficient and attractive opportunities for people to meet, talk, and share together.

15. *Be accessible to employees.* Establish easy-to-use channels of communication, both formal and informal. Make sure they are kept open and communicate real, salient information about the company and the department. Do management by walking about. This does not mean sending lots of emails. It means being physically and psychologically accessible, within reason. It means not punishing those who want to meet you.

16. *Ask employees for their feedback and their ideas.* Involve them in decisions that affect their jobs. Reward them for good ideas that, when implemented, improve both individual and group efficiency. Genuinely listen to them—most of them are at the coalface. Publicize the rewards given to those with good ideas.

17. *Use good performance appraisals and behavioral measures as major criteria for promotion.* Collect good data on input. Make it clear that rewards are contingent on progress and that equity principles apply in the organization.

3

Money messages, moneygrams, and money muddles

INTRODUCTION

This chapter is about where money irrationality and igno-rance come from and how to prevent them. It deals with the issue of how to introduce children, adolescents, and young people to the economic world to try to ensure they behave wisely and rationally and with respect to both their, and others', money.

Moneygrams are parentally sent messages (telegrams) about money: The shoulds and the shouldn'ts. Money messages sent by parents are about how children see money being used to express mistrust or suspicion, about how it is used to foster family alliances and exclude members. Children observe what their parents say and do, which can often be contradictory. The money issue is often so emotionally charged that children may either adopt parental money attitudes and behaviors or completely reject them. Thus the highly stingy, hoarding parent can beget children with very similar money-security-based tendencies, or children who spend money with gay abandon, known by everyone as wild spendthrifts.

Some parents, particularly the rich who have made their own fortune, need to apply effort and ability to ensure there is not the "gutter to the gutter in two generations" effect. That is, these people have come from nowhere and do not want their children to waste their fortunes. Many of these people attribute their personal success to their own personal money beliefs and behaviors. And they want their children to share them. They can be very strict, often making great demands of their children to work for their pocket money. They are very clear about the messages they want to send to their children, which they believe will put them in good stead for later in life.

Children first learn that money is magical. It has the power to build and destroy and to do literally anything. Every need, every whim, every fantasy, can be fulfilled by money. One can control and manipulate others with the power of money. And it can be used to protect oneself totally like a potent amulet. Money can also heal both the body and the soul. Money opens doors. It talks loudly. It can shout but also whisper. And its influence is omnipresent. It is a tool and weapon.

But legends, films, and books suggest that it can also corrupt. It can be black magic. People sell their souls for dirty money. Too much money can corrupt; it can mean a loss of control. It can be a drug and a destroyer.

Adults also often believe money is a panacea for all problems—lots of money, lots of solutions. It has magnetism and seemingly a cause of insatiable and an unquenchable thirst. But those who eventually acquire money at some cost often feel disappointed, let down, even betrayed by the myth.

Is the money-hungry adult the manifestation of the deprived child? Hunger, greed, envy, and guilt are all powerfully associated with money at all ages.

MONEY DISORDERS AND FAMILY DISORDERS

Do your money problems and attitudes result from your childhood? Did the moneygrams you received from your parents account for any present problems? Consider this checklist that may help identify whether this is the case (Matthews 1991):

1. Were your parents extremely secretive about money matters? Are you still in the dark regarding how much money your parents have (or had)?
2. Did your parents argue about money frequently?
3. Do you collude with any other family members to keep certain financial information from other members?
4. Do you believe you have absorbed a fear of poverty from your parents, though you've never been in real financial danger?
5. Do you feel like a fraud when you are in the company of your family, even if the rest of the world considers you a bona fide success?
6. Do you find yourself frequently complaining about financial mistreatment by a parent or sibling?
7. Is one of the siblings in your family the designated "success," while others seem unable to unwilling to succeed economically?
8. Do you sometimes conceptualize your financial actions (spending, saving, and so on) in terms of "being good" or "being bad"?
9. Do your parents use money to reward and punish you even now when you are an adult?
10. Do your parents send you money unexpectedly and expect certain prescribed gestures of affection in return?
11. Is it difficult for you to imagine outdoing your parents financially?
12. Do you frequently find yourself acting exactly the opposite way with money from your parents (for example, do you spend flagrantly where they scrimp avidly)?
13. Was there any type of compulsive behavior in your family of origin, for instance, alcoholism, drug use, overeating?

14. Was it "understood" in your family that money was a male domain?
15. Do you notice that money is used to communicate the same emotional messages in your marriage as it did in your family of origin?

Money disorders are learnt from "family disorders." The messages families send about money are, however, simultaneously overt and covert, and often paradoxical, inconsistent, and confusing. Parents can, and do, express their feelings towards their children through money: reinforcing good habits and success at school. They can bribe and withhold, they can spoil and deprive, and they can openly discuss or remain very secretive about money.

In most cultures women have had much less opportunity than men to handle significant sums of money. Boys often negotiate pocket money and allowances with the father, though girls may be encouraged to charm their fathers into opening their wallets. Hence some girls come to believe that financial wheeling and dealing is a masculine activity, and shun all money matters for fear that it renders them somehow less feminine. On the other hand, if boys equate having, spending, and "flashing" money with masculinity they can feel very inadequate in the company of others with money, or overspend what they don't have as a means of making a statement about their masculinity. These sex differences may be on the decline in the West, but they are still strong in the developing world.

But some children respond to parental messages by doing the precise opposite. Financially over-cautious parents spawn profligate and imprudent children. Other children attempt to outdo or exaggerate the financial behaviors of their parents. Some people appear completely indifferent to money and unworldly. A common theme running through their money attitudes is that they do not deserve it. Inevitably, those who believe they do not deserve a fair financial return for their labors will not receive it.

Yet as well as early and later childhood experiences, inevitably cultural values and habits prescribe and proscribe money related behavior. Societal values dictate what is rich and what is poor; how money should be made; on what one's disposable income should be spent; who are monetary heroes and anti-heroes. Schools formally and informally teach financial attitudes and habits. Equally, the media tend to reinforce culturally acceptable money values and habits, which naturally appear a little bizarre to cultured travelers. All societies also have their messages about money sacrificing, donations, and gifts to others.

Healthy, happy, economically-knowledgeable parents beget children who (hopefully) understand economic reality and act both responsibly and wisely when it comes to money. All parents make errors, but there are simple rules about bribery, inconsistency, and secrecy that can help matters.

There are well-known stages in thinking development when children are able to understand about specific money concepts (profit, budget, interest) and to acquire skills. Often they know more about where babies come from than how bank interest or the free market works.

Adults, some in therapy for money-related problems, but also those with few worries, easily recount messages they got from their parents. These may be implicit or explicit, but they remain powerful determinants of the adults' thinking and emotions about money.

Money messages adults reported getting from their parents

- If I tell somebody how little I earn then he or she will view me differently.
- My friendships are threatened if I start earning a lot more or a lot less money.
- My father worried, but did not talk, about money the whole time.
- My mother cheered herself up by shopping.
- My parents insisted on having separate bank accounts.
- Nobody told me the real financial status of our family.
- I was often ashamed about how comparatively poor we were.
- Most fights between my parents involved money.
- Our family had lots of money secrets.
- I was shocked to find, later in life, my beliefs about our family's poverty/wealth were completely wrong.
- My parents were more concerned about the places I worked rather than the money I earned.
- My father prided himself on being a "good provider" for his children.
- I was told my pocket money was a privilege, not a right.
- My father gave gifts not to symbolize love but to provide substitutes for it.

Parents can do sensible things for themselves and their children. These include buying enough insurance, saving for their retirement and their children's education, making (and where appropriate revising) a will, and enjoying their money.

It is unwise to think of yourself, or behave, as if you are an accountant or a social worker, a manager or a genie.

Your job is simply to educate and model the behavior that you want.

EDUCATIONAL ISSUES

The sorts of issues parents ask and worry about are:

- Whether to attempt to turn shopping trips even for pre-schoolers into educational expeditions.
- Whether, and how, to watch (and openly critique) television together, especially advertisements.
- The business about starting and negotiating the rules for pocket money and allowances.
- Whether to reward good grades/marks at school with extra pocket money.
- How best to encourage sensible saving.
- When, and how, to open a bank account for their children.
- Whether to get children interested in the stock market so as to raise a City of London/Wall Street whiz kid.
- Whether to encourage or discourage collecting (hoarding) of things (that is, junk).
- Whether to encourage their children to do odd jobs (babysitting, gardening, cleaning) for friends, neighbors, and/or strangers for money.
- What sort of part-time job to encourage their children to seek.
- Whether to encourage voluntary (unpaid) work over paid work.
- Whether to encourage or discourage family and friends giving money or gifts for birthdays and other celebrations.

- How best to save, insure, and invest money for their children to secure for them a good future (that is, setting up trusts; reducing inheritance tax).
- Whether to give or loan their university/college-age children money for education, housing, cars, and so on.
- How to treat the post-university, without-a-job returnees: That is, whether to charge them rent, and what house rules to set.
- What to do as a grandparent or step-parent or guardian as opposed to a parent.

These are important issues. They may have very important consequences. Parents (rightly) worry about them, or they should. And it is not always clear where they can get good helpful, practical advice.

Before secondary (high school) it is possible to educate children about economic issues. Topics include:

- *Profit*: What are profits? Are they necessary? How much do businesses make? Where do profits go?
- *Jobs*: Where do they come from? Who chooses who and why? Why do people change jobs? Who makes the decisions about how much a job is worth and how?
- *Competition*: What is it? Is it good for us? Is it fair? Who benefits?
- *Taxes*: Why do we pay them? Who pays and when? How is the money spent? What are the alternatives?
- *Inflation*: What causes prices to go up? What does it do to individuals and families?
- *Savings*: Why save? How much should people save?

Where is the best place to save money? If I borrow money, how much interest do I pay?

- *Investing*: How can I best invest my money? What are stocks and shares? How are these bought and sold?
- *Starting a business*: What do I need to know? What do I need to do?
- *Advertising*: What is it for? How does it work? What happens if it is stopped or banned?

One of the most powerful and probably primitive of urges is for parents to pass on wealth, possessions, and wisdom to their children. Parents are prepared to make extensive extended sacrifices for their children. It is genetically determined, deep-seated and hardwired. Any government whose inheritance tax hits too many—beware!

All parents want their children to be financially literate and financially sensible. Some have other hopes for children, like taking over the family business from them. Many self-made men and women hope their children will "continue their legacy"; "build on what they created"; even "consolidate their gains." But many are disappointed. Many fortunes gained with considerable effort, financial acumen, and well-calculated risks are lost by indolent, spoilt children.

Studies of successful entrepreneurs, bankrupt spendthrifts, and obsessional savers often point to childhood experiences as drivers. Some of those money beliefs and behaviors developed serendipitously. Sometimes they were in direct response to specific events (for example, sudden loss of wealth in the family, or death of a parent). Sometimes they were the direct result of parental training.

ALLOWANCES, POCKET MONEY, AND FAMILY RULES

Adults often have powerful memories about how their allowance system worked. Some never got allowances at all. Others had to "work for them." Some parents had strict rules about what they could and could not spend the money on. Some report that pocket money could be stopped as a punishment; or increased as a reward.

Money messages come from parents, peers, relatives, and wider society. Parents' religious beliefs can impact powerfully on their money beliefs. Equally children learn a lot from social comparison and how they "stack up" compared with closest friends and acquaintances.

Often children who have, and get, everything they want neither understand money nor respect those who gave it to them. The spoilt brat is not money-smart or money-wise. Parents, it is argued, can set up for themselves potential time bombs in the way they socialize their children.

Janet Bodnar, whose book *Dr Tightwad's Money-Smart Kids* (1993) is subtitled *Teach your kids sound values for wiser savings, earning, spending, and investing,* suggests ten things *not* to teach your children:

1. *Ignoring the whole topic*: because of embarrassment, fear, or ignorance not discussing money openly and honestly.
2. *Indulging your children*: for guilt, or shame, or any other problem.
3. *Sending mixed messages*: about saving and spending, waste and profligacy, restraint and impulsivity.

4. *Being inconsistent*: setting money rules and then breaking them.
5. *Not setting up a system at all*: instituting early rules.
6. *Using verbal platitudes instead of practices*: being cynical and sarcastic rather than giving good advice.
7. *Failing to educate and listen*: not answering their questions, or not giving good answers.
8. *Reliving your childhood*: not understanding about the changes in the current cost of things.
9. *Informational overload*: the opposite of 1, by not understanding when, why, and what to say.
10. *Complaining* about your job: making the world of work seem unpleasant or like slavery.

SENDING THE RIGHT MESSAGE

As children grow in their understanding of, and interaction with, the adult world they can be introduced to money. But what should parents do and how?

There are many different pocket money or allowance systems to choose from. Pocket money may be given as often as it is requested or needed; as a salary for work around the house; with strings/responsibilities attached; with no strings attached; or as supervised (versus freedom of choice) pocket money.

Parents have to think about when to start (and change) the system, how much to give, rules about when it is given, for what, and what to do about it. They need to explain and model the concept of budgeting.

The following rules and recommendations have been distilled from many books on the topic, all of which are aimed at parents.

Children aged 3–7

- Provide children with tools to save (such as transparent piggy banks).
- Play with real or fake money: Count, stack, and guess the cost/value of things.
- Describe the difference between needs and wants (food versus ice-cream; medicine versus a CD player) frequently.
- Encourage coin identification and change calculations at home and in shops. This is both fun and useful.
- Start pocket money as early as 3–4 years old, but explain what it is for.
- Make pocket money related to behavior (that is, specific chores completed appropriately and on time, such as gardening, cleaning, and tidying). Over time children become responsible for their own jobs and job charts.
- Explain why children cannot have certain items they ask for (costs too much, money ran out). Be as straightforward as possible, realizing they might not understand certain things.
- Use coins to rehearse arithmetic problems.
- Try to help children divide money into spend and save piles regularly and wisely.
- Take children shopping and explain your decision making. Be sensible yourself!
- Discuss contents, values, and options of different goods when shopping, particularly in supermarkets and department stores.
- Let children watch your money transactions (that is, how to receive, calculate, query change).
- Explain and set up a budget for childhood money (lunch, bus fare, school trips, breakages).

- Introduce the concept of citizen of the household and what responsibilities are (sharing, giving, honesty).

Children aged 7–12

- Get children interested in banking and formal savings. Explain how banks work. Go to the bank with them, read leaflets and open an account/s. Yes, as young as seven years old.
- Let children read about their investments, if they have any (bank statements/share certificates).
- Encourage children to have a (big) long-term (six months to a year) savings goal.
- Show children family bills (food, rent, insurance) and explain them fully.
- Explain and model charity giving, and encourage your child to do likewise.
- Establish rules for "gift money" from others at Christmas, birthdays, and so on.
- Explain issues like tipping, tolls, tokens, consumer rights, value for money, comparative shopping.
- Buy and explain a consumer magazine and how it works.
- Watch and/or read television commercials together, and analyze them for motive, product value, and technique.
- Explain tax (income and VAT) and tax your children's pocket money (say 10 percent) to have a family tax where the whole family both contributes and decides how to spend it. Family meetings should be called to discuss this.
- Lay down rules (with explanations) for borrowing, lending, and trading both within and outside the family.

- Explain the use of verbal and written contracts about money related issues (such as payback after loans).
- Establish rules/policies about breakages, money found on the street, mistaken over/under payments, and shoplifting.

Teenagers (13 years old and upwards)

- Encourage, model, and educate in the use of debit and credit cards.
- Encourage personal and Internet banking. Discuss and calculate interest with them.
- Direct debit pocket money into their accounts, perhaps as a standing order.
- Make them personally and totally responsible for their own bills—especially clothes, mobile phones, and computers.
- If you loan them money, agree and stick to reasonable repayment terms (period and interest).
- Charge them board and lodgings if they have an income from part-time work.
- Help them save wisely—that is, discuss where best conditions are to be found.
- Encourage regular, sensible, and thoughtful budgeting.
- Explain the stock market and together play with a set amount (for instance, £100). Start a portfolio, even at 13 or 14 years old.
- Show and explain family insurance policies, schemes, and payments.
- Explain the concept of a will and the details of your will specifically with respect to financial implications.
- Discuss your income honestly and how you spend it.
- Encourage smart consumerism: keeping receipts,

knowing rights, understanding shop sales, knowing store return policies, reading the labels.

- Discuss entrepreneurship and opportunities to supplement income.
- Encourage your child to do part-time (Saturday) jobs.
- Ask for evidence of budgeting plans and decisions.

Does all this sound difficult or impossible? Does it all seem too much or too embarrassing? What is surprising is that modern parents seem to be able to discuss sex, drugs, and the like, but neglect money issues. Some recognize that money education is a very wise investment against future problems.

Remember you send messages whether you like it or not.

MONEY DECISIONS

Clever people make bad money decisions. Educated business people do not follow the rules of economics and mathematics. The heart can so easily rule the head.

Psychologists have twice won the Nobel Prize for economics. In 2004 Daniel Kahineman was awarded the prize for his groundbreaking work on behavioral economics. This is the science of everyday economics. It looks at the reasons people borrow, invest, save, spend—and waste money. It attempts to answer simple but important questions like:

1. Why do people put money in banks and building societies when the interest rates they get are below that of inflation? Are they trading off security for loss? Do they understand what they are doing?

2. Why are people willing to spend more on a product they purchase with a credit card than if they pay cash?

3. Why do people sell shares just before they skyrocket but hold onto poorly performing stocks and bonds?

4. Why do people seem to seek out and remember money details that are in favor of their ideas and forget all those that go against their own theories?

5. Why are people so confident and optimistic about their own abilities to keep and expand their wealth? Why do most believe they are above average and that economic misfortune is more likely to befall others?

6. Why do people believe that they have so much control over their personal economic affairs that they can personally and powerfully influence financial outcomes?

7 Why do wealthy middle-class people get into debt?

People categorize, label, or segregate money depending where it comes from and how it's spent. Spending with credit cards seems different from cash. Spending a tax refund may be done casually, even recklessly, but spending the same amount of their post-tax salary seems quite different.

Money is money, is money. Assuming it is legally acquired, it all spends in the same way. It is irrational to treat it differently depending on its origins. And it really is good advice about looking after the pennies and letting the pounds look after themselves.

People are certainly sensitive to loss. Consider the following two situations. In both you are given £2,500. In the first you have two choices: you can take an extra £750 or flip a coin and win or lose £1,500. In the second situation, you either lose £750, or can flip a coin and lose

£1,500 or nothing. Most people show they are more willing to take risks to avoid losses and are more conservative in securing profits.

Somehow the difference between £0 and £1,000 is greater than that between £1,000 and £2,000. So losing £2,000 is not as proportionally as painful as losing £1,000. And equally gaining £2,000 is not twice as enjoyable as winning £1,000.

People have different emotions when thinking about gains and losses. Many of us are over-sensitive to loss. Signs of this are whether you make spending decisions heavily influenced by how much you have already spent. Equally it is a sign if you sell winning investments more readily, when confronted with losses.

Various researchers have rejoiced in listing the manifold errors that people make when thinking about or investing their money. All this research is based on cognitive psychological research. Hilton (1998) lists seven deadly sins:

1. *Confirmation bias*: People seek information that confirms rather than disconfirms their beliefs, hunches, and hypotheses. Those who are best able to make money are least able to resist this bias. There is a great deal of information about money, trends, and productivity. It is dangerous and foolhardy to seek out only those statistics that support their views. Theories need to be tested. People need to search out disconfirming data. It is better to try to find information about money (investment, productivity) that proves them wrong. This bias is of course not only confined to money issues, it can also have serious consequences when big investment decisions are involved.

2. *Optimism bias*: Most people believe they are above average: better drivers, more intelligent, healthier, and more law-abiding. This cannot be true. Also they believe they have more control over their personal outcomes than others. In short, people are optimistic and have the illusion of control. This may be healthy but it can make for really bad economic decisions. The weather, political insecurities in far-off countries, election results, can all play havoc with the stock markets over which people have little or no control.

3. *Overconfidence in prediction*: Success has its drawbacks. It tends to make people over-confident. People can be and are over-confident in their economic predictions for many reasons. Past success and the availability of lots of information are not necessarily guarantees of wise decision making.

4. *Risk aversion*: We all like certainty. Most of us would like to live in a stable, orderly, predictable world where things are both clear and certain. We know that people become risk-seeking when confronted by losses.

5. *Regret aversion*: Here people anticipate loss they behave over-cautiously. Curiously people feel more regret if they change shares/bonds than if they do not, even if they don't lose the same amount of money. The status quo appears overly attractive in decision making.

6. *Mental rigidity*: People tend to over- and under-react when making money decisions. Some go with the trend (momentum strategies) while others try to buck the trend (contrarian strategies). The former might be a good idea in the short term and the latter in the long term, but both show inflexibility.

7. *Mental accounting bias*: This refers to all the human factors that influence decisions—values, preferences,

and memories. It also refers to the social context within which people make decisions. Decision making is often a social process.

Others have tried to provide sound advice to people about not falling into the many traps associated with faulty reasoning about money (Belsky and Gilovich 1999).

Imagine getting a check for £1,000 either from a lottery win, a tax refund, or a salary increase. Will you spend it differently? Is gift money different from earned money? Is "luck money" different from invested money? The rational answer is "no."

People have a natural aversion to loss. The question is whether this badly influences their financial decision making and their taste for risk. Good strategies for coping with this include diversification, focusing on the big picture, and trying to forget the past.

People stay in unsatisfying jobs because of their investment in getting the job in the first place (such as in training). They spend more and more money repairing things because they have already spent lots on them. We endure bad books, movies, and videos because we have spent good money on them, not because they are good. People waste time, money, and effort justifying the past (in therapy). You make better money decisions by looking at the present, not the past, and by considering what things are worth now, not what they were worth in the past.

Money decisions can be difficult. Deciding not to decide is of course a decision in itself. Some people however show extreme confidence in their ability to predict a bargain and to negotiate.

Belsky and Gilovich (1999) say that over-confidence may cost you money if:

- You make large spending decisions without much research.
- You take heart from winning investments but "explain away" poor ones.
- You think you are "beating the market" consistently.
- You make frequent trades, especially with a discount or online brokerage.
- You think selling your home without a broker is smart and easy.
- You don't know the rate of return on your investments.
- You believe that investing in what you know is a guarantee of success.

What the researchers have shown is that people often follow simple rules. They call these heuristics—logical short cuts that often lead people to be short-changed. The wise and the well informed are aware of these foibles and try to avoid them.

So the point is this:

- All money is the same. Do not treat it differently depending on where it comes from, where it's kept, how it's spent.
- Losses hurt people more than gains please them. Loss aversion reduces risks.
- Money that is spent is money that doesn't matter. The sunk cost fallacy can make one a victim of the past.
- Decisions depend on the way you look at the problems: on how problems are framed.
- Bigness bias means small numbers are not treated as wisely as big numbers.
- People pay too much attention to specific things and ignore others.

- Hubris is a seductive trap of the knowledgeable and confident.
- It's hard to admit mistakes and break patterns of thought or behavior.
- A trend may not be your friend: it can lead to herd investing.
- You can know too much: too much information can confuse more than illuminate.

Good investment advice is not difficult to find. Do your homework: Understand the fundamentals. Invest in companies/sectors you know and understand. Be a specialist: Don't follow the whole market. Beware fads, fashions, and hot tips. Diversify. Calculate and understand your risk. Buy low (in gloom), and sell high (in bloom), which is easier said than done. Money decisions are, it seems, not like other decisions.

We are prone to lots of biases. It is probably healthy to be optimistic and self-confident, but that can lead to bad money decisions. Studying the evidence, weighing up the risk, learning from experience, all sounds straightforward but the evidence suggests it's not that easy when it comes to our own money. But the good news is we can be trained to be more logical. Just as we can, should, and do train our children to understand the economic world and the world of money, so we can train ourselves and other adults to make better, wiser, money-related decisions.

CONCLUSION

All parents want to teach their children to be sensible with money. Many want to ensure their children do not make the same mistakes that they did. They want to bring up children with a respect and understanding of all economic issues, the real value of money, and the role it plays in life. Children learn by observation as much as by instruction. It's best to think clearly about this issue and to set in place some simple but important practices.

Asked what emotions people most associate with money, the following is a typical list. Note the order:

1. Anxiety.
2. Depression.
3. Happiness.
4. Anger.
5. Envy.
6. Excitement.
7. Helplessness.
8. Resentment.
9. Fear.
10. Guilt.

It is clear that negative emotions tend to overwhelm positive ones. Money issues confuse and upset people. Just as Victorians seemed unable to talk about sex, so modern parents struggle when talking about money. Many suspect, quite rightly, that they can have a great impact on their children's subsequent money-related behavior. They can, in short, shape children's money beliefs and behaviors via the messages they send.

Of course other images about money can be found in the media. The electronic and print media have always found it easy to have images of the rich and poor.

FIGURE 3.1 RICH AND POOR,
GOOD AND BAD

	Good	Bad
Rich	Philanthropic	Greedy
	Noblesse oblige	Manipulative
	Caring	Corrupt
Poor	Honest, deprived,	Lazy, feckless,
	widowed,	criminal,
	orphaned, sick	undeserving

The media makes us believe that:

- Buying things or having things makes people happy.
- Looking fashionable and wearing the latest styles is really important.
- One way you can tell who is cool and who isn't is by the things a person owns and the clothes a person wears.
- Nobody has to work very hard to have nice things.
- It's possible both to have a lot of nice things and to have lots of free time to spend with your family.
- People who do have to worry about those things usually find simple solutions to their problems.
- There is usually a good reason why one person has money and another doesn't. There's nothing unfair about it.

We are products, not prisoners of our own past. Our parents, relatives, teachers, and government have sent us implicit and explicit, straightforward and ambiguous, simple and complex messages about money: How to get it and keep it, how to use it, and what it stands for. Young people, more so in the West than in less-developed countries, remain profoundly ignorant about many aspects of the economy, to their own cost. And the escapism, sensationalism, and trivializations of the media do not help! Just as we want healthy and literate young people, so we want them to be economically savvy, wise with money, and appreciative of its uses, abuses, and power.

4

Money on the couch

INTRODUCTION

Money is at the heart of some relatively serious mental problems. People get into a great deal of trouble through the way they store, spend, and save money. It can easily break relationships. It can also lead to very bad work-related decisions.

Money self-help books give advice to the money troubled. Most is sensible and sound, if a little unsurprising. These books advise the money obsessed or money troubled to do some pretty obvious and sensible things. The sorts of issues are usually these:

1. Do a sensible, realistic audit of what you have, where you are, and so on.
2. Specify as clearly (and realistically) as possible what you want, where you want to be, and why.
3. Analyze your feelings about, and explanations for (they are inevitably related) how you have got to where you are (money-wise) and why you want to be somewhere else.
4. Specify the forces preventing and encouraging you to achieve your goals.
5. List all the options that you have and the possible implications of different decisions.
6. Make real choices for today and live in the present.
7. Understand the importance of planning for the future.
8. Get on with it, and redo (the analysis/audit). Run the checks regularly (say annually).

More important is the issue of decision-making styles with respect to money. Who makes what decisions, when, and about what? Does one partner make the big money implication decisions (those with a big total cost) and the other partner the smaller decisions? Does one make spending and other saving/investment decisions? Who, and when, and why, and how do couples seek (independent) financial advice? Who decides about charity/philanthropic giving? Who decides on where, and by whom, and why money is stored/kept/banked/invested?

All therapists talk of communication patterns or styles among couples. It becomes particularly interesting when opposite money types are involved or working together: miser versus spender; worrier or repressor; victim versus victimizer. Inevitably various techniques, rules, hints, and/or advice steps are suggested, which are well known to all counselors and therapists. One approach is to start with your "money history" by trying to explain to your partner the story of your experience of money as well as goal setting.

Essentially it means talking more (explicitly, openly, regularly) about money; sharing the load and responsibility for decisions; having agreed budgets and goals; and having an agreement on the big picture and long-term goals.

RETAIL THERAPY, POOH, AND PARSIMONY

Early Freudians noticed the association in everyday language between money and filth/faeces. People becomes "stinking rich" and maybe (hopefully) "rolling in it." They look forward to accumulating "filthy lucre" but not being "cleaned out." They hope to "make a pile."

The Freudian explanation is that our attitudes to money are formed in the anal phase of development. This also determines our attitude to time, to waste, to cleanliness, and to parsimony. And it may explain why people go shopping when depressed to "pick themselves up."

The psychoanalytic theory goes something like this.

1. All children find instinctual libidinal pleasure in the expulsion of faecal matter. In short it is natural to enjoy defecation.
2. This process meets a variety of reactions from other people depending on their personality, culture, and so on. They go from horror to humor.
3. The most typical response is to subject the child to some type of toilet training procedure. This occurs in all cultures but with different rules that carers may have. They can be rigid or lax, idiosyncratic or systematic.
4 Parents ecstatically praise the child when he or she defecates in the prescribed receptacle and may try threats and punishment when he or she does not. The range of behaviors is wide.
5. During this period, the child is also striving to achieve autonomy and a sense of self-worth. The child senses control over the parents as they try to control him or her on the potty.
6. Toilet training may then become a battleground in which there is a power struggle between child and parents, a conflict as to whether the child feels in control of sphincter muscles or feels compelled to submit to parental demands out of fear of punishment or threat of loss of love.
7. Children are thought to have extensive and often distorted fantasies about their faeces; there may be

great pride because the faeces are a creation out of their own bodies; their expulsion may represent bodily mutilation, or be confused with giving birth, as a mother does. Most children want to examine and play with their faeces, which horrifies parents. After all, children believe they made them and they belong to them.

8. These fantasies are influenced to a degree by feedback from the environment, but the likelihood of perceptual distortion remains high because of children's limited experience and limited intellectual understanding.

9. Confusion is typically amplified if parents express great pleasure with the faeces the child deposits in the potty, treat it like a gift of gold, and then later communicate that it is dirty and smells bad. It is disposed of as immediately as it is received. The faeces are objects of fascination to the child. The children after all made them, faeces vary, and apparently they are really important. But they seem to have to be given away and "junked." So there is a pleasure in holding back (keeping them and possibly displeasing the parents) rather than freely and easily giving them on demand.

10. Parents may encourage the child to defecate at a particular time (after meals) and in a particular place. They may place a great store on hygiene before, during, and after the event. Hence the association of money with order, cleanliness, procrastination, and so on.

11. Many parents will give enthusiastic praise (unconditional positive reward) when their child obeys.

12. Gradually the child learns sphincter control, and house (and culture) rules about defecation. When and where and how you pooh are shaped by parental demand.

13. But—and here is the leap—attitudes to authority, cleanliness, health, money, possessions, and time are shaped powerfully and unconsciously at the time. The more children are "traumatized" by strict or peculiar potty training, the more they are scarred for life and likely to be anal.

The anal adult—the anal personality—may be a parsimonious miser, respectful of authority, on time, and very orderly. This type of person has learnt that submission to parental authority (in elimination of faeces) leads to approval and affection. And thus diarrhoea, constipation, and irritable bowel syndrome are all seen to be, in adults, imbued with psychological significance. So the miser is defiant in the face of parental demands. The spendthrift is eager to obtain parental approval.

What implication does all this have for the world of work? Assuming the Freudian analysis has some truth in it, the following may be deduced. *First* and foremost our attitudes to, and uses of, money are often unconscious and deeply imbued with emotion. This naturally makes them very difficult to change. *Second*, change is deeply threatening partly because money attitudes are closely linked to other phenomena like attitudes to time and order.

The description "anal character" is bandied about in everyday language. People smile at employees who insist on keeping their office or cubicle completely orderly and neat. Anal characters can become radically upset by things that are misfiled. They like things to be filed and piled, checked and correct. They may therefore be attracted to jobs that call for these traits. Health and safety, quality control, time keeping, and waste-management suit anal characters. Interestingly anal types pooh-pooh the values, beliefs, and practices of those different from them.

As they rise in the organization anal characters may try to impose their needs and preferences on others. They feel comfortable, secure, and productive under particular conditions. They may select others in their own image, and believe that the way in which they prefer to do things is normal, healthy, and adaptive. They may of course be right or wrong depending on their excesses.

Zealous anal characters may have strong needs to impose their preferred way of doing things on others. They have usually a series of clever rationalizations for why things have to be done in a particular way, even if they have little insight into them.

The bottom line is this: anal characters have a constellation of related traits that reflect their beliefs, preferences, and behaviors. Thus they tend to be orderly, punctual, obstinate, and concerned with cleanliness. They can be seen to be mean. They withhold not only money from others, but other things of value like information and feelings. Attitudes to money are just one feature of the "syndrome." There are famous cases like the US billionaire Howard Hughes who demonstrated all the traits associated with the (obsessive-compulsive) syndrome.

Freudians emphasize both the role of instinctual drives and the origin of irrational or peculiar adult behavior lying in forgotten behavior learnt in early childhood. But social and cultural influence must play a part. Growing up in poverty surrounded by the rich or vice versa inevitably has an impact. Being brought up in the icy cold waters of Puritan philosophy will certainly have an impact. This can easily lead to guilt feelings about either or both of having or not having money.

Freudians argue that people can experience and deal with the guilt both consciously and unconsciously. People can give their money away by being great benefactors or donors. They can make restitution to, and even seek forgiveness from, those they feel they have exploited. But unconscious guilt can lead to depression, to psychosomatic illnesses, and to self-punishment. It is not always clear to individuals why they have such a strong desire (or indeed no desire at all) to amass great wealth and at the same time the desire to get rid of it recklessly.

MONEY TYPES

There are many popular books describing money types. They nearly all suggest that their behavior is caused by *falsely equating money with something else.* It is assumed that people have consistent beliefs, fantasies, and behaviors with respect to their money—how they save, spend, invest, and so on. It is nearly always assumed that these patterns develop in childhood and are maintained throughout adulthood. That is, like a personality trait they are stable over time and consistent over situations: "Always a miser," "forever a spendthrift," "an eternal irrational hoarder."

We can become money wasters, money chasers, money avoiders, money prudes, and money Midases. "Good money types" can be categorized as:

- virtuous scrimper
- generous charitable donor
- shrewd investor
- vigilant bargain hunter

- benevolent giver
- contented pauper.

"Bad money types" can be categorized as:

- unlucky gambler
- chronic borrower
- corner-cutting petty cheat
- flashy spender
- profligate waster.

Money does certainly mean different things to different people. It is a status symbol in nearly all cultures. But it also has powerful psychological meanings. Various clinicians have tried to isolate, describe, explain, and then treat various money types (Forman 1987; Goldberg and Lewis 1978).

- *Security manifest in the Safety First Syndrome.* This is where emotional security is confused with financial security. Money helps some people cope with, and fend off, anxiety in what they see as a dangerous, fickle world. They feel vulnerable and frightened. Money gives them self-assurance, confidence, and decisiveness. They can feel hurt and rejected, but even worse, worry that others will deprive them of their money— their primary defense.
- *Power manifest in the Green Giant Syndrome.* This is the motivator of top management: to dominate, control, and direct. Money, it is believed, clears away objects, it overpowers others, and it provides immense advantage in the struggle for superiority. It may be related to infantile experiences of omnipotence and the desire to force others to stay with the individual and do (all) his

or her bidding. But the power-oriented seem never to get enough power through money, and become very greedy. Omnipotence comes at a cost.

■ *Love manifest in the Santa Claus Syndrome.* The emotionally uninhibited or those feeling emotionally deprived use money to buy love via presents. The love-starved feel they have little to give and therefore get little in return. They seek money to give it away, in turn reciprocally, to acquire love. Money then, is a gauge of emotional worth and caring.

■ *Freedom manifest in the Declaration of Independence Syndrome.* Paradoxically the pursuit of money enslaves people in order to supposedly help them gain freedom. These people imprison themselves in jobs and relationships that they do not like so that they can get enough money to break free and do what they really want. Hence the concept of "golden handcuffs." Freedom lovers seek money to buy time to do what they really want to do. Money is the means to do whatever they want to do, wherever they want to do it, including seeking revenge, comfort, acquiring knowledge, and having sex.

■ *Self-worth manifest in the Compensation Syndrome.* Money makes people feel important. It hides feelings of inadequacy. It makes people believe they are really worthwhile. Wheeling and dealing; conspicuous consumption, and flashing money about can make people feel very important. They can be admired however short, ugly, and talentless they feel themselves to be.

It is certainly worth exploring these types in more depth. Therapists often note that those seeking help

with emotional problems have highlighted the importance of money issues. The way people think about and
use their money can cause them and those about them
considerable money problems.

Hoarders, misers, security collectors

The psychology of hoarders is familiar to all novelists. They
make good characters as epitomized in Dickens's Scrooge.
These people supposedly distrust people, the world, and
the future. They put their trust in money and their money
in trust. Having and keeping money, it is believed, reduces
their feelings of insecurity and dependence. Hoarders
seem to come in four forms:

- *Compulsive savers.* For them saving is its own reward.
  They in effect tax themselves and no amount of money
  saved is ever sufficient to provide enough security.
  Some even become vulnerable to physical illness
  because they deny themselves sufficient heat, lighting,
  or healthy food. They are always insecure about how
  much money they have. They are strongly compelled to
  do without, to acquire ever-larger amounts of money to
  be totally safe.
- *Self-deniers.* These types tend to be savers but enjoy the
  self-sacrificial nature of self-imposed poverty. They
  may spend money on others, however, though not
  much, to emphasize their martyrdom. Psychoanalysts
  point out that their behavior is often a disguise for envy,
  hostility, and resentment towards those who are better
  off. "Take my last cent/penny. I can do without it," they
  have been heard to cry. "I will enjoy my poverty."
- *Compulsive bargain hunters.* Money is fanatically

retained until the situation is "ideal" and then joyfully given over to acquire real bargains. The thrill is in outsmarting others—both those selling and those paying the full price. The feeling of triumph often has to validate the irrationality of the purchase, which may not really be wanted. But they get short-changed because they focus on price, not quality. They tend to know the price of everything, but the value of nothing. And they can waste so much time and effort (and petrol) chasing a bargain, that it would be much more rational for them to work a little longer and pay full price.

- *Fanatical collectors.* Obsessed collectors accumulate all sorts of things, some without much intrinsic value (bus tickets, beer mats, trivial ephemera). They can become famous and important for what they possess, appearing on daytime and children's television programs. Their collection can bring them fame and security. They turn to material possessions rather than humans as potential sources of affection and security. They acquire more and more but are reluctant to let anything go. Collectors can give their lives a sense of purpose and avoid feelings of loneliness and isolation. Objects are undemanding, and well-known collections can bring a sense of superiority and power.

All of these types are trying to remain safe. They pursue money, which they see as safety, instead of happiness, success, or productivity. They fear trusting others with their emotions. They trust things, not people, and fear dependency. They see people as coy, capricious, irascible, and undependable. They mourn, they self-punish. They are secretive about their money and have difficulties with relationships because money is a barrier to close friendships.

Ten symptoms and typical reflections of misers

- All my life I have hoarded money. My family and friends have often commented on how much money I have stashed away.

- I am fascinated by money. I often hold onto funds rather than spend them, even though there is no particular reason to do so.

- I don't usually admit to being niggardly. As a matter of fact, I am likely to justify my miserliness as being necessary, foresightful and virtuous.

- I have a terrible fear of losing funds and of being taken advantage of financially. Although I am often envious of other people's wealth, I tend to keep these feelings inside.

- I have trouble enjoying the benefits of money and tend not to have much fun with cash. I'll spend money on necessities, but I resent using it for other purposes.

- My friends and family are often angry with me about how little money I spend.

- I don't know why I behave in a miserly way, although I usually tell myself it's for the money. I store money as a way to reduce my discomfort and anxiety, but I don't know what causes these feelings.

- When someone asks why I behave as I do about money I reply, "I feel as though something terrible is going to happen to me if I keep spending my money," or "I feel secure only when I hold onto my money."

- I have difficulty trusting others and am often competitive. This trait makes it difficult for me to get along with people in general, not only in money matters.

- I sometimes fail to take care of my health as well as I might because of my penny-pinching.

Source: Forman 1987, pp.20–1.

The treatment, of course, is dealing with anxiety (about weaknesses and dependency). Apprehensiveness and mistrust are at the roots of miserly behavior. Once this is addressed the irrational beliefs about the protective power of money can be confronted. Some treatments not only encourage but also actually demand that money is spent from a deliberately set up "anti-miserly" account.

Penny-pinching behavior is resistant to change but can be both confronted and cured. Some nations (like Scotland) have a reputation for "crafty tightness" with regard to money. Some Scots rejoice in this stereotype, others profoundly reject it. But it does suggest that social forces, particularly religious beliefs and economic forces, play their part in determining money pathology. Seeing other people die rich and their money go to the state is often a useful "wake-up call" to the miser.

Love, friendship, and passion

The psychoanalytically inclined researchers Goldberg and Lewis (1978) hypothesized that:

> Money is often given as a substitute for emotion and affection. Money is used to buy affection, loyalty and self-worth. Further, because of the reciprocity principle inherent in gift giving, many assume that reciprocated gifts are a token of love and caring. Money can be used to acquire, indeed, trade in emotions.

They list three classic types:

■ *Love buyers.* Many attempt to buy love and respect: those who visit prostitutes, those who ostentatiously give to charity, and those who spoil their children. They feel unloved but not unlovable, and avoid feelings of rejection and worthlessness by pleasing others with their generosity. Thus they need to acquire large sums of money to give away. However, they may have difficulty reciprocating love, or their generosity may disguise true feelings of hostility towards those they depend on. Again the paradox: excessive giving may disguise real hating.

- *Love sellers.* They promise affection, devotion, and endearment for inflating others' egos. They can feign all sorts of responses and are quite naturally particularly attracted to love buyers. Some have argued psychotherapy is a love buyer–seller business transaction open to the laws of supply and demand. The buyers purchase "friendships" sold happily by the therapist. Love sellers may gravitate to the caring professions. Perhaps the new fad for business coaching is precisely this phenomenon. The businessperson is buying love and respect, the coach is selling it.
- *Love stealers.* Kleptomaniacs are not indiscriminate thieves but those who seek out objects of symbolic value to them. They are hungry for love but don't feel they deserve it. They attempt to take the risk out of loving, and their being generous is very much liked, but they tend only to have very superficial relationships.

Overall, then, it seems that whereas parents provide money for their children because they love them, parents of potential love dealers give money *instead* of love. Because they have never learnt to give or accept love freely they feel compelled to buy, sell, or steal it. The buying, selling, trading, and stealing of love is, for Freudians, a defense against true emotional commitment, which must be the only cure.

Spendthrifts are often trying to acquire love, admiration, and relationships rather than possessions. They often say they feel hollow or empty, and hope that spending money (or even stealing goods) will solve their problems. Many spendthrifts have a poor self-image and low self-esteem. They are rash and irresponsible with money spending, which can cause embarrassment, guilt, and debt. They may be trying to say, "Take care of me or save me." An over-indulgent and overprotected childhood means that these people learn that money is a substitute for affection. Spending is an indulgence and it can strengthen their identity.

Shopping has been made easy, so compulsive spenders are on the rise. But there are self-help groups that meet to discuss their problems and to think about how they sabotage themselves by destructive spending.

The materialist society of "to have is to be" only encourages spendthrift compulsiveness. As an extreme it has been suggested that some people even equate money with immortality: that spending money is a denial of death.

Power grabbers and spenders

Money, to some people, can mean power, poverty, humiliation, and weakness. These people see the world as win–lose, dog-eat-dog. They are cynical about others and are easily enraged by being thwarted. They believe having and understanding money effectively gives them power over others. Three money types who are essentially power grabbers are:

Ten classic symptoms of compulsive spenders

- My spending is frequently compulsive and out of control. I need to spend the way an addict needs a fix. I feel the need to spend continuously and often go on sprees or binges. I usually have little interest in the things after they are purchased, however.
- I frequently run up large debts and I use my credit cards liberally. If I have any money left over at the end of the month, I usually spend it.
- I often need to spend money when I feel depressed, under stress, worthless, afraid of being hurt, being alone, or being rejected.
- I often spend money as a way of providing instant gratification when what I actually want is love, recognition, or admiration.
- When I buy things I feel positive about myself, but it never lasts. After it's all over, I go back to feeling guilty and unworthy.
- I can't stop myself from spending, even though I feel guilt or shame afterwards.
- My family and friends are often annoyed and hurt by my overspending.
- My spending problem is not serious, but I do tend to rely on credit cards and to pay only the minimum balance due. I also buy things on credit that I wouldn't buy when paying cash and I often don't have enough money around for emergencies.
- Although I don't understand the real underlying anxieties, fears, and concerns that fuel my overspending, I often think that I could get out of debt if only I had more money.
- Spending money makes me feel good in a way nothing else does.

Source: Forman 1987, p.32.

■ *Manipulators of other people.* These people use money to exploit vanity and greed in others. Manipulating other people makes these types feel less helpless and frustrated, and they feel no qualms about taking advantage of other people. Many lead exciting lives, but their relationships present problems as they fail or fade due to insult, repeated indignities, or neglect. Their greatest long-time loss is integrity. They get a reputation for trying to buy favor, respect, indeed the very souls of others. They rarely succeed of course; particularly with those they respect most, which is their primary frustration.

■ *Business empire builders.* They have (or appear to have) an overriding sense of independence and self-reliance. Repressing or denying their own dependency needs, they may try to make other people dependent on them. Many of them inevitably become isolated and alienated, particularly in their declining years. Their behavior in attempting to hold onto power can look ever more pathetic and senseless.

■ *Godfathers.* They have more money to bribe and control so as to feel dominant. They often hide anger and a great over-sensitivity to being humiliated— hence the importance of public respect. But because they buy loyalty and devotion they tend to attract the weak and the insecure. They destroy initiative and independence in others and are left surrounded by second-rate sycophants.

Power grabbers felt rage, rather than fear, as children, and express anger as adults. Security collectors withdraw, psychotherapists argue, with fear; but power-grabbers attack. Victims of power grabbers feel ineffectual and insecure, and get a pay-off by attaching themselves to someone they see as strong and capable. They may therefore follow "winners," particularly if they have enough money. Power grabbers are driven, manic, obsessed. They clearly do not have a realistic perception of money.

Ten classic symptoms of "Tycoon trauma"

- I am not very interested in spending money, but I love to amass it.
- Even when I have more money than I need, I still work at increasing my stockpiles.
- For as long as I can remember, I have been interested in making money.
- I am always looking over my shoulder to find out if I am doing better than others.
- I rarely think about what money will buy for me. As a matter of fact, sometimes I wonder what it is all about.
- My family resents my absorption with moneymaking.
- When I am not involved in money, I often feel anxious for no reason.
- Sometimes I worry that I am too absorbed with making money, but I soon forget about it when I realize how well I blend in with others who do the same thing.
- I often think that the more money I have, the better control I'll have over my world and the happier I'll be. At other times, I think I'm doing all this for my family, so when there's enough money I'll be able to be with them. I'll stop working then
- Money is the best way to gain power, status, and approval.

Source: Forman 1987, pp. 40–1.

Another version of this malady are the *bargain hunters*. They are the kings of the haggling process. They believe that paying the full price for anything is both a personal affront and a serious defeat. They are thrilled by the process and the battle of wits. They see a lowering of the price by sellers as a caring act, or at least one of respect.

Bargain hunters can be terribly irrational. The process becomes more important than the product. The game is

---

Ten symptoms of bargain hunters

- When I shop, I must feel that I'm saving money and that the price was less than usual.
- I enjoy knowing that others pay more for things.
- I can't resist a sale of almost any kind and I often end up buying things just because they are bargains. Many of these purchases get little or no use.
- The thought of paying the full price for anything revolts me.
- As a child, I felt emotionally short-changed. When I find a bargain, I feel that someone cares for me.
- Getting things for less money makes me feel superior. I sometimes feel a desperate need to be treated in this special way.
- Getting a great deal helps me alleviate feelings of insecurity and vulnerability.
- I spend a lot of time, energy and thought on my money-saving pursuits.
- I can't stand paying the asking price for anything. It makes me feel bad about myself if I do.
- I feel that there's something wrong with me if I can't get the seller to come down significantly in price.

Source: Forman 1987, p. 49.

---

more important than the end result. For the psychoanalyst the aggressive competitiveness of bargain hunters is evidence of attempts to protect themselves against possible rejection. Outsmarting others lowers anxiety. The idea is to get something (love, of course) without having to buy it or pay the full price.

Freedom, autonomy, paradise

Money can buy freedom but it can also cause enslavement. For many in the West it is a necessary evil: a hard-gotten but acceptable passport to autonomy.

This belief is the more acceptable, and hence more frequently "admitted" meaning attached to money. Money, it is believed, buys time to pursue one's whims and interests, and frees one from the daily routine and restrictions of a paid job. There are two sorts of autonomy worshippers:

- *Freedom buyers.* For them, money buys escape from orders, commands, even suggestions that appear to restrict autonomy and limit independence. They want independence, not love: in fact they repress, and hence have a strong fear of, dependency urges. There is the paradox again. They fantasize that it may be possible to have a relationship with another "free spirit" in which both of them can experience freedom and togetherness simultaneously. They are frequently seen as undependable and irresponsible, and can make those in any sort of relationship with them frustrated, hurt, and angry.
- *Freedom fighters.* They reject money and materialism as they think it is the cause of the enslavement of

many people. Frequently political radicals, dropouts, or technocrats, they are often passive–aggressive and attempt to resolve internal conflicts and confused values. Camaraderie and companionship are the main rewards for joining the anti-money forces. Again, idealism is seen as a defense against feeling. There may be a large cost if these people get involved with political or religious cults that have ideological stances with respect to money. These people are the eco-warriors of today.

An underlying theme here is that dependency on other people and on the world early in life was perceived as a threatening rather than a rewarding experience. This observation is based on clinical observations and interpreted through the terminology of a particular theory.

TREATMENT AND THERAPY

There are all sorts of potential treatments for the money-insane, money-neurotics, and the irrational abusers of money. These treatments include cognitive behavior therapy. The idea is to look at money beliefs, over-generalizations, and "black-and-white" thinking about money. The technique is to examine negative perception, faulty labels, and jumping to conclusions. The ultimate aim is to examine, uncover, confront, and change automatic thoughts about money, and to replace these irrational thoughts with rational ones.

Some believe in relaxation therapy for dealing with the money anxious or assertiveness training with the money timid. Psychodynamic therapists ask people to examine their psychohistory of money and see the links between money hang-ups and early history. The idea is to break the link between how adults behave irrationally with respect to their money to satisfy unmet or frustrated needs of childhood.

Many therapists, advisors, or trainers believe in the value of letting go emotional baggage from the past, forgiving, and accepting the present. A good start is to look at people's values and associations with money.

But as well as dealing with the past there are things to be learnt about the present. These include how to budget and how to save. The idea is to look at compulsive over- or under-savers and how unconscious thoughts and emotional factors are inhibiting reason.

The same is true of dealing with insurance, which can be associated with a fear of death. Some people become phobic even having to think about different kinds of life insurance, writing a will, or indeed (and more under-standably) dealing with their taxes.

Adults need to understand their investments, however modest. They need to know about sane investments, risk, credit cards, credit ratings, and the real cost of borrowing.

The money-content know what money can and cannot buy. They can usually distinguish between material desires and emotional needs. Money can be thought about and used logically. It does not need to lead to anger, anxiety, envy, and rage. People need to achieve self-confidence and a good self-image without attempting to buy them. People need to feel loved, respected, and independent for who they are, rather than the money they have or spend. Above all people need to be rational money managers, not gamblers, impulsive spendthrifts, or miserly hoarders.

Interestingly the different money types, not unnaturally,

seek out therapists who fulfill their particular needs. Thus, those concerned with authority will seek out a less conventional therapist (money related), while the security collector will be attracted to the least expensive therapist in the local market. Because (nearly) all therapists charge money for their services (though there is not necessarily any relationship between cost and quality of treatment), entering psychotherapy means spending money on oneself. Yet money remains a relatively taboo subject between therapist and client. Clearly, all therapists need to understand the shared meaning attached to payment and non-payment for services throughout the course of therapy. Also, paying shows commitment. Withheld payment is seen as a sign of displeasure. Forgetting to sign or date a check can also be easily interpreted.

Psychotherapists believe that money beliefs and behaviors are not isolated psychic phenomena but integral to the person as a whole. People who withhold money may have tendencies to withhold praise, affection, or information from others. People who are anxious about their financial state may have something to learn about a fear of dependency or envy. Therapists attempt to help people understand their money madness. Money can become the focus of fantasies, fears, and wishes, and is closely related to denials, distortions, impulses, and defense against impulses.

For all psychoanalytically inclined clinicians the money personality is part pleasure-seeking, frustration-avoiding id, part reasonable and rational ego, part overseeing, moral, superego. This accounts for the oft-reported but curious paradox of seeing people lethargic and depressed after a major win and elated, even virtuous, after financial depletion.

Rather than typologies of money madness (such as neurotic saver or spendthrift), some psychologists see a continuum from mild eccentricities with subtle symptoms through *moderate* money neurosis to *full-blown* money madness. Money in the circumstances of money madness:

- can be used to express mistrust and suspicion
- can be used to foster alliances between family members and to exclude other members
- can instigate manipulation
- can cause projection of emotion and blame
- frequently can be invoked as an instrument of control
- can be used to foster unnatural dependencies
- can be used to assuage parental guilt
- can be offered in lieu of heartfelt apology
- can be used to express boundary problems, which occur when family members cannot quite tell where *their* money problems end and someone else's money problems begin.

Therapists believe there is a host of reasons why people run so easily into debt. People may buy too many things that boost their capacity for self-esteem, or to try to fulfill a fantasy they have about themselves. Some may get into serious debt out of an unconscious desire to impoverish themselves, or to get rid of their money because on some level they find it loathsome. Alternatively, people may "overdebt" because they feel unfulfilled and frustrated in some significant aspect of their lives and because spending temporarily takes their minds off their sense of emptiness and unhappy circumstances. People may overdebt because compulsive behavior of one sort or another runs in their family, or as a reaction against a family or origin where thriftiness was excessively prized. People may overdebt to try to keep up with their peers, or because they are unable to resist media messages which instruct them to "shop till you drop" (Matthews 1991).

There are "pack thinking" (conformity of views) investors who play stock markets and whose greed and belief in eccentric experts can lead to spectacular monetary successes and failures. Economic shamans, the stars, and superstitions all appear to play a major role in a highly capricious and unpredictable world. Many behave quite irrationally to allay feelings of uncertainty and insecurity about financial matters.

So how do you know if you are "money healthy"? How do you know if you are cured? The answer, says Matthews (1991), is to admit or recognize the laws of money. The more you believe these statements are true, the more your behavior reflects them, then the more money sane you are:

- Money is neither god nor devil. But in this world it is a necessity.
- Money can be used constructively or destructively.
- Money can symbolize anything we wish it to.
- Money is not time. Time is time.
- Much of the way we behave toward money is unconsciously motivated.
- Money is safest when it is "out of the closet," discussed calmly and candidly with your spouse, your parents, and, most especially, your children.
- A degree of detachment from money is desirable. A disdain for money is detrimental.

- In order to have enough money so that you do not have to think about it, you must think about it.
- Those who feel they don't deserve to have much money usually don't.
- Those who will not share some of their money suffer emotional and social consequences.
- Those who only take and do not "make" money suffer emotional and social consequences.
- Where money is given there is expectation.
- Where money is taken there is obligation.
- Love goes better when partners know that love is not money.
- Work goes better when money is a by-product of work and not the principal motivation to work.
- We are not what we earn, own, or owe. We are what we are.

MONEY IN RELATIONSHIPS

Money can be a problem in all relationships; parent–child, spouses, lovers (especially divorcees); employer–employee; flatmates; landlord–tenant. This is particularly the case where individuals seem to have opposite beliefs and values; one person sees money as the source of happiness, another as a source of misery and corruption; one is avoidant, in denial, repressive of money talk, the other talks about it constantly; one enjoys risk, the other is terrified of it. Some couples have happy, harmonious money relationships. They share similar values and take a hopefully rational view. Some see money as a tool, others as a weapon.

Money is deeply symbolic: it carries powerful emotional charges. It can tangibly represent control, independence, freedom, love, power, security, and self-worth. Money can be associated with morals. But money itself, an economist always tells us, is neutral. What is not neutral is how we spend or use it.

One hot question is, are there consistent, explicable (and perhaps harmful) sex differences around money? Is there a male culture and a female culture of money? One argument goes that the two sexes are socialized differently: women to be sharing, caring, and cooperative, men to be tough, successful, and competitive. Women (it is said) are (more) comfortable about expressing their feelings, even vulnerability, while men cannot, do not, and believe they should not. Men are encouraged to be thinking types, women feeling types. Men must be competent, independent, and self-confident.

If this is true (or even true-ish), these differences can very easily and powerfully impact on differences in how the sexes approach money. Men usually (often, still) earn more money, and are supposed to act with social confidence. Women and men may therefore have different attribution patterns of assigning blame and taking credit for money success (men, others; women, themselves). They probably harbor different fears about money as well as different fantasies about its power and effects.

As a result, women can easily be in dependent relationships at work. They might withdraw from financial affairs, being convinced that they can't understand or influence them. Hence they may endure very unsatisfying personal relationships if they feel they at least provide them with the security of money. Equally they can become addicted to irrational, compulsive, emotionally driven money behavior, particularly spending. As a result, some women may not charge the "going rate" or "appropriate worth" for their work. Worse, they may not pay others appropriately, partly because they believe that money defines their worthiness as individuals.

Money can have a profound effect on friendships. Most of us are attracted to people with similar backgrounds and values. Further, at work people choose *where* to work and the organization chooses *them*. This can mean that at work there is a great deal of homogeneity, with people being very like each other in terms of attitudes, personality, and values.

However, it is quite possible, indeed probable, that people do not share similar behavior and attitudes to money. Thus one person might be a saver, the other a spender. One person might be very open about money, the other secretive. People may (incorrectly) assume that others think and feel (about money) just as they do.

Borrowing and lending between family and friends is fraught with problems. The major problem is that people find it difficult being explicit or even worse drawing up (even an informal) contract about what they have, in effect, agreed. People rarely consider or talk about simple ground rules, what they jointly understand. Friends and family have expectations and make assumptions about each other. They tend to be helpful, to show generosity or cooperativeness, to "buy" approval or forgiveness, or just to ensure peace and quiet. When asked to lend money they may not be able to say "No."

And what of the perspective of the borrower? Does the borrower know when and how the loan will be repaid, in part or in full? Is it a gift, interest-free, or with (what) interest? Is the act of having or wanting to be a borrower demeaning? Should the borrower be expected to put up collateral if it is a big loan? Could the borrower ever imagine being taken to court if the loan was not repaid to the friend or family member?

Advice is pretty simple. If you don't want to go down the written contract route (which is probably preferable), then at least have an open discussion about expectations of the repayment and think about some ground rules. Stick to the agreement. If problems arise the issue needs to be discussed and renegotiated, just as you would do with a bank manager.

People cannot or should not complain about a "loan" not being repaid if there are no ground rules established in the first place.

An additional complication for families is the intergenerational transfer of wealth. Some parents encourage their children to believe that "one day" all that is theirs will go to their children. That is, those children can count on inheriting a property, a nest egg, and an investment portfolio. But people live longer and things change. Quite simply the more people believe they are entitled to inherit from their parents or get constant, unconditional help and assistance, the less likely they are to take full responsibility for their own finances.

Money is always a big issue in divorce. Differences and disagreements about money and sex are commonly cited as major causes of divorce. Couples attend to, organize, and agree their money affairs differently. But if advice and recommendations are to be given, then couples should consider the following:

■ Discuss money issues (particularly gifts, loans, fees) openly, honestly, and regularly. Put the issue "on the table" from the start.

- Settle the issue of separate and joint accounts; how the system works; who pays for what, when, and why.
- Designate who organizes what affairs, investments, insurance, daily accounts.
- Keep tabs on where money is kept, and what is coming in and going out. Touch base, revisit issues.
- Accept and encourage odd expenses and personal passions; allow each person in the relationship to spend certain amounts precisely as he or she wants to.
- Agree an amount (for example, £1,000) above which money decisions have to be discussed jointly.
- Talk openly but privately and never in public about these issues.
- Sing from the same "hymn-sheet" when it comes to children. Don't confuse them, hide issues from them, or have a "do as I say, not as I do" philosophy.
- Regularly revisit money goals and targets; discuss them honestly and revise them with feedback.
- Beware of social comparison; concentrate on what you as a couple prefer to work on, not on what others do. Work out what you really want and need to do, not just what the neighbors do.
- Never use money as a weapon; never blackmail; divorce money from emotions as much as possible.
- Use trusted money advisers and both go to meetings with them.

Certainly, there are many, and very emotional, issues following relationships/marriage break ups and/or divorce. There are step-parent issues, problems with ex-partners, and child-support payments.

MONEY MADNESS MEASURES

Goldberg and Lewis (1978, pp.100–1) suggest the following (informed; non-psychometrical) test of money sanity.
The more you tick "Always," the greater is your problem.

	Always	Sometimes	Never
1. You put money ahead of everything else in life, including health, love, family, recreation, friendship and contentment.	___	___	___
2. You buy things you don't need or don't want because they are on sale.	___	___	___
3. You buy things you don't need or want because they are the "right" things to have, or because they might impress others.	___	___	___
4. Even when you have sufficient funds you feel guilty about spending money for necessities such as a new pair of shoes.	___	___	___
5. Every time you make a major purchase, you "know" you are being taken advantage of.	___	___	___
6. You spend money freely, even foolishly, on others but grudgingly on yourself.	___	___	___
7. You automatically say, "I can't afford it," whether you can or not.	___	___	___

	Always	Sometimes	Never
8. You know to the penny how much money you have in your purse or pocket at all times.	____	____	____
9. You have difficulty making decisions about spending money regardless of the amount.	____	____	____
10. You feel compelled to argue or complain about the cost of almost everything you buy.	____	____	____
11. You insist on paying more than your share of restaurant checks or bar bills just to be appreciated or to make sure that you do not feel indebted to anyone.	____	____	____
12. If you have money left over at the end of the month, you feel uncomfortable until you spend it.	____	____	____
13. You use money as a weapon to control or intimidate those who frustrate you.	____	____	____
14. You feel inferior to others who have more money that you, even when you know they have done nothing of worth to get it.	____	____	____
15. You feel superior to those who have less money than you, regardless of their abilities and achievements.	____	____	____
16. You firmly believe that money can solve all your problems.	____	____	____

	Always	Sometimes	Never
17. You feel anxious and defensive when asked about your personal finances.	___	___	___
18. In making any purchase, for any purpose, your first consideration is the cost.	___	___	___
19. You feel "dumb" if you pay a little more for something than your neighbor did.	___	___	___
20. You feel a disdain for money and look down on those who have it.	___	___	___
21. You prefer saving money to investing it because you're never sure when things will collapse on you and you'll need the cash.	___	___	___
22. The amount you have saved is never quite enough.	___	___	___
23. You feel that money is the only thing you can really count on.	___	___	___

Money sanity measure

Forman (1987, pp. 9–10) offered a simple test of your money sanity. Again indicate the extent to which you do the following: the more frequently you tick "Always," the less healthy and sane you are:

	Always	Sometimes	Never
1. Do you find yourself worrying about spending, using, or giving money all the time?	____	____	____
2. Are you inhibited about talking to others about money, particularly about your income?	____	____	____
3. Do you buy things you don't really need because they are great bargains?	____	____	____
4. Do you lie awake at night trying to figure out a way to spend less money and save more, even though you are already saving money?	____	____	____
5. Do you hold on to or hoard your money?	____	____	____
6. Do you regularly exceed the spending limit on your credit card?	____	____	____
7. Does gambling make you feel a burst of excitement?	____	____	____
8. Would you walk blocks out of your way to save a bus fare you could easily afford?	____	____	____

	Always	Sometimes	Never
9. Are you constantly puzzled about where your money goes or why there is none left at the end of each month?	___	___	___
10. Do you use money to control or manipulate others?			
11. Do you refuse to take money seriously?	___	___	___
12. Do you resent having to pay the full price for any item when you shop?	___	___	___
13. Do you often gamble and spend large sums on your bets?	___	___	___
14. Do you spend a large proportion of your free time shopping?	___	___	___
15. When you ask for money, are you flooded with guilt or anxiety?	___	___	___
16. Are you increasingly anxious about whether you can pay your bills each month?	___	___	___
17. Do you spend money on others but have problems spending it on yourself?	___	___	___
18. Do you buy things when you feel anxious, bored, upset, depressed, or angry?	___	___	___
19. Are you reluctant to learn about practical money matters?	___	___	___
20. Do you think about your finances all the time?	___	___	___

Money malady measure

Matthews (1991, pp. 232–4) suggested 25 questions that tap into your faulty money attitudes. The more you agree or feel, think, feel, or behave like this regularly, the more problems you have:

		Always	Sometimes	Never
1.	Do you feel compelled to act a certain way toward money, even when part of yourself knows that to do so is not in our best interests?	___	___	___
2.	Do you believe your loved ones would describe you as "inflexible" when it comes to money matters?	___	___	___
3.	Is the first thing that comes to mind when someone suggests altering your behavior toward money the thought, "'I can't, I can't"?	___	___	___
4.	Do you become enraged at people whose money-related behavior is the opposite of your own (if you are a saver, do you rail at spenders and vice versa)?	___	___	___
5.	Do you find yourself frequently accusing others of the kind of extreme financial behavior others have accused you of?	___	___	___

	Always	*Sometimes*	*Never*
6. Do you notice an extreme reluctance on your part to discuss your money or money behavior with anyone?	___	___	___
7. Do you believe that if people knew the truth about your financial life they wouldn't love or respect you anymore?	___	___	___
8. When faced with a financial problem, do you feel utterly helpless and paralyzed?	___	___	___
9. Do you tend to ignore financial problems until they become extremely serious?	___	___	___
10. Are you petrified at the thought of making any money-related decision for fear it will be the wrong one?	___	___	___
11. Does this trio of traits describe you: extremely frugal, exceedingly stubborn, and preoccupied with order and cleanliness?	___	___	___
12. Do you have persistent fears that someone, somehow will manage to take your money away and "ruin" you? And are you obsessed with financial prophylaxis—taking every conceivable precaution to preserve your assets?	___	___	___

	Always	Sometimes	Never

13. Do you feel utterly incapable of enjoying money? Do you experience feelings of shame, guilt, disgust, or disdain in connection with it? ____ ____ ____

14. Do you believe it is "wrong" to buy a luxury item even if you can easily afford it? ____ ____ ____

15. Are you extremely bitter and cynical about giving money (for example, do you refuse to give a pound to a homeless man because "he'll buy wine"; do you refuse to donate to charity because "the money gets stolen by the bureaucrats")? ____ ____ ____

16. Or are you the polar opposite of frugal—given to spending money impulsively without much thought as to whether you really need or even want what you buy? ____ ____ ____

17. Would you call your desire for money "insatiable"? ____ ____ ____

18. Do you believe there is a certain amount of money that will provide happiness? Do you keep revising the amount upward? ____ ____ ____

19. Once you reach a financial goal you set for yourself, do you then feel let down and disappointed, as if something were missing? ____ ____ ____

	Always	Sometimes	Never
20. In general, do you consider yourself an addictive personality?	___	___	___
21. Do infusions of money make you ebullient, while losses make you extremely forlorn?	___	___	___
22. Do you repeatedly find yourself in situations where you are broke or flush, with few in-betweens?	___	___	___
23. Do you feel much more self-possessed when you are in possession of money than when funds are low?	___	___	___
24. Do you experience a great deal of anxiety in relation to the comings and goings of money?	___	___	___
25. Do you torment yourself by conjuring up scenarios in which you envisage yourself destitute and helpless?	___	___	___

Earlier, Matthews (1991, pp. 222–9) offered a shorter quiz, again, the more you tick "Always," the greater is your problem:

	Always	*Sometimes*	*Never*
1. Do you find yourself scrutinizing new acquaintances to see what kind of plates they serve dinner on, what color credit card they use in a restaurant, whether or not they wear designer clothes, and whether their jewelry is real or costume?	___	___	___
2. Do you notice yourself feeling superior or inferior to them based on the results of your "survey"?	___	___	___
3. Have you ever found yourself dressing in such a manner as to "fool" people into thinking you are wealthier than you actually are?	___	___	___
4. Do you feel duped when you discover that someone who communicates, "I am wealthy" through dress and demeanor turns out to be less well off than you suspected?	___	___	___
5. Have you ever caught yourself behaving obsequiously toward a person known to have a great deal of money?	___	___	___

	Always	Sometimes	Never
6. Do you frequently watch television shows and read magazine articles that feature profiles of the rich and famous?	___	___	___
7. Do most of your friends make as much money or more money than you? Have less financially successful friends tended to fall by the wayside as your income increases?	___	___	___
8. Do you attempt to "keep up with the Joneses" even when you know that doing so will jeopardize your financial security?	___	___	___
9. Does a day rarely go by when you do not find yourself envying others for things they have bought with their money?	___	___	___
10. Do you feel gratified when you know that someone envies you for material advantages you may possess?	___	___	___
11. Do you consider yourself easily influenced by advertising?	___	___	___
12. Do you believe that name-brand products are always superior to generic products?	___	___	___

	Always	Sometimes	Never
13. Do you enjoy being in situations where you are the target of sales pitches (for example, do you tune into Home Shopping Network; do you peruse most of the ads in magazines)?	____	____	____
14. Can you be easily pressured into making a charitable donation you don't really want to make if a neighbor, colleague, or employer of yours solicits you?	____	____	____
15. Have you ever given more than you could really spare to a charitable cause in order to "save face" in your community?	____	____	____
16. Have you ever borrowed money (say, on a line of credit attached to one of your credit cards) in order to make a donation?	____	____	____

CONCLUSION

The number and complexity of the factors influencing the way people make money related decisions is nicely illustrated by Wilson (1999, pp. 106–7). Figure 4.1 sets out this interactive picture: internal predispositions, unconsciously formed in early childhood, are reinforced (or reacted against) under parental influences over the ensuing years into young adulthood. The three main aspects of this more conscious level of parental influence are:

- the atmosphere surrounding money (unspoken messages such as silence and prudence)
- specific (spoken) admonitions and maxims about money
- money action (behavior observed and experienced by the child).

From this the individual develops a propensity to be primarily a saver or a spender, the key variable involved being control. Anxiety levels reflect the extent to which the predisposition and the sense of control feel under threat. Predispositions may also have a bearing on other personality variables such as optimism, externality, self-esteem, competence, efficacy, and so on. These, in turn, affect outcomes in the saving–spending balancing act.

FIGURE 4.1 PERSONAL MONEY ATTITUDES: INPUTS AND OUTCOMES HOW WE EACH ARRIVED AT THE SAVING—SPENDING POSITION

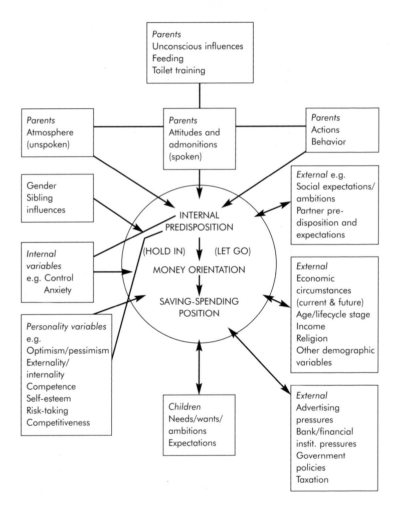

5

Money in society

INTRODUCTION

What do religions teach us about money? Is wealth linked to political beliefs? Indeed what do different political groups think about money?

This chapter looks at these questions. But it begins with the fundamental and vexed relationship between money and happiness.

MONEY AND HAPPINESS

Does happiness come with being financially well off? Can we buy happiness? When asked what would improve the quality of our lives, for most people the first answer would be "More money." Yet researchers in the area have showed that there is only a modest correlation between income and happiness. This is, for economists, deeply threatening, for it is given wisdom and indeed axiomatic that people pursue things that are in their interests. We are on a *happiness treadmill* because once we have got what we want it no longer makes us happy. Within most affluent countries people with lots of money are (only) somewhat happier than those with just enough to afford life's necessities. Of course people in rich countries are somewhat happier than those in poor countries. And those who have lots of money are happier, at least for a time.

So what do we know about happiness, the causes and consequences? Most people everywhere report slight to moderate happiness. People's moods certainly go up and down but their natural level of happiness remains very stable. Personality factors are very important determinants of happiness, more so than money. Stable extroverts are consistently happier than neurotic introverts. Happiness it seems is also partly genetically determined.

People's level of happiness is surprisingly robust. Even after a major negative experience—unemployment, death of spouse, even being made quadriplegic—or a major positive experience—winning the lottery or the birth of a child— a person's "natural level" of happiness returns. A great amount of money has only a very short-lived consequence.

Comparing oneself with others (health, wealth, physical status) does affect happiness but not exclusively so. The factors that best predict happiness are (in order):

- physical and mental health
- healthy social relationships especially within the family
- a satisfying job
- a sense of values and goals (often religion) as well as a stable personality
- being an active and valued member of a community.

Money makes a bigger difference in poorer societies. But materialism—the valuing of money and possessions above relationships—is negatively correlated with happiness. During the last 50 years, the average US citizen's buying power has more than doubled. It is not quite as much in Europe, but it is a lot. The 1957 per-person after tax income inflated to 1995 US dollars, was $8,500; by 2002, thanks partly to the rich getting richer and to women's increasing employment, it was $23,000.

Did this more than doubled wealth—enabling twice as many cars per person, and TVs, laptops, cell phones—also buy more happiness? Are those of us who enjoy the abundance of the affluent Western world happier? The average US citizen, though certainly richer, is not happier. In 1957, some 35 percent said they were "very happy," however by 2002 the figure had fallen to 30 percent. Happiness is determined quite clearly by things other than money. It may however, be quite another thing for the determination of unhappiness. There is no reason to assume that these findings would not be the same in Europe.

What *really* makes people happy? Money is quite well down the list. Having good close friends, a supportive loving relationship or marriage, good health, and a connection to other groups in the community counts more than money.

Taking Figure 5.1, longitudinal data collected for over 70 years in the West shows a linear rise in personal income (such that it doubles every 30 years) but a flat, horizontal line for self-reported happiness/well-being, suggesting little or no difference over time. We are twice as rich as we were 50 years ago, but only about as happy. The results seem to suggest that, at least after a certain point, there is no relationship between personal wealth and happiness.

However there are some interesting caveats. The first is that *relative wealth* is important. If my wealth rises faster than yours, I am likely to be happier than if yours rises at the same rate. Reducing the salary of others has the same positive effect as increasing my salary!

However aggregated data such as this may easily obscure important differences between individuals, between organizations, and between countries. At the individual difference level there is considerable accumulating evidence that happiness is related to stable, biologically based personality traits (extroversion and stability). This suggests that happiness is stable over a lifetime, in part because people with particular personality profiles seek out and change situations to fit their personalities.

FIGURE 5.1 AMERICAN TRENDS

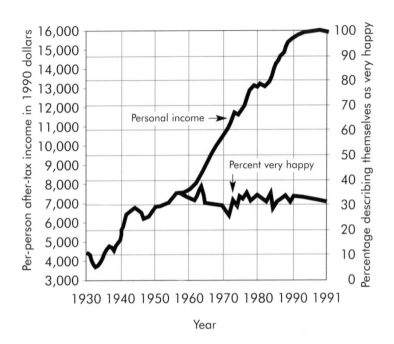

Source: National Opinion Research Center happiness data from Richard Gene Niemi, John Mueller, and Tom W. Smith, *Trends in Public Opinion: A Compendium of Survey Data* (New York: Greenwood Press, 1989); and from Tom W. Smith (personal communication). Income data from *Historical Statistics of the U.S., Colonial Times to 1970*, pt. 1 (Washington DC: Bureau of the Census, 1976), p. 225, and *Economic Indicators* (November 1980): 6 and (November 1991): 6, adjusted to 1991 dollars. From Myers (1992).

But it does seem to be the case that people in some organizations seem overall (and quite consistently) to be happier than others because:

- they are paid more
- they have much better conditions, management, and prospects
- some organizations attract happy people

- the organization tends to be more successful
- all of the above
- none of the above.

Organizations differ widely in structure, process, and product as well as culture, mission, and vision. Because corporate culture is an implicit but powerful force it can have an effect on the manifestations or suppression of many values in the workplace. Some organizations seem happy to acknowledge the spiritual dimension to life while others find it faintly embarrassing. To some money means everything, others downplay it.

At the third level—namely cultural/national—there are also interesting differences. History, geography, language, and religion as well as economic development all have a part to play in the quality and quantity of materialism in a culture. Countries differ most obviously in their wealth, which has been linked to a national feeling of well-being. However it is never clear in cross-cultural correlation studies whether wealth leads to happiness, or vice versa, or the relationship (or lack of it) is moderated by a third variable, such as social cohesion, or political and economic stability.

There are also consistent national differences in happiness. Inglehart (1990) reported an extensive study with representative samples of 170,000 people in 16 nations. Results indicated that first, there are genuine national differences. For example, the Danes, Swiss, Irish, and Dutch felt happier and more satisfied with life than did the French, Greeks, Italians, and (West) Germans. Second, the nations' well-being differences correlated modestly with national affluence, but the link between national affluence and well-being was not consistent. In fact there was no clear statistical relationship or trend. For instance, for the French, the average income was almost double that of the Irish, but the Irish were happier.

However, there is more than one fact that makes the nations differ in self-reported happiness. For instance, the most prosperous nations have enjoyed stable democratic governments, and there is a strong link between a history of democracy and national well-being. Moreover, countries that have both democracy and a free press also tend to have happier people. The freedom in choosing type of job, the workplace, and one's own lifestyle, which are associated with democracy, may also be contributors to individual happiness. So living in a democratic country and having jobs and lifestyles to choose from counts for a lot in terms of happiness.

But within any country are the richest the happiest? Again, there is a modest link between happiness and being financially well off. Those who live in affluent countries yet have low incomes, clearly live with less joy and more stress than do those who live with the comfort and security of higher incomes.

One study reported that income correlated with human rights and with the equality within nations 0.80 and 0.84, respectively (Deiner, Deiner, and Deiner 1995). Besides, individualism is a cultural variable that correlates across nations with both higher reported happiness and higher suicide rates.

But having more than enough provides little additional boost to happiness. The question, of course, is what is more than enough? One plausible reason is that low income is a strong predictor of negative affect (emotion) but not positive affect (emotional reaction). However the best predictor of happiness is the balance of positive and negative.

However, there is much evidence for the moderate association between wealth and happiness. There are many sound theoretical reasons why this may be so. These include adaptation level theory (one soon adapts to wealth at any level), social comparison theory (one's comparison group changes so that one never feels rich), and the marginal declining utility of money. *Yet the idea that money brings happiness remains pervasive.*

It could be that how people actually perceive their money is important to individual happiness. There are essentially two explanations for the frequently established finding that except for the seriously poor, money only buys temporary happiness. The first is the *adaptation level principle*, which means judging the new by the old. If we get richer we get initial pleasure but soon adapt to it. It becomes the norm, it becomes commonplace. We need more to have the effect again. Satisfaction and happiness are all relative to recent experience. People quickly recalibrate. Thus to seek happiness through money requires a very great deal of it: an ever-increasing amount.

The second principle is the *relative deprivation principle*, which refers to the fact that happiness is relative. As people get richer they change their comparison group so they never feel rich. Paradoxically people can be made happy by others becoming poorer as much as by themselves becoming richer. If we compare ourselves with the better off we experience envy, but if we compare ourselves with poor people we can (hopefully) count our blessings. We tend to do neither but do compare ourselves with our peers. And if they change as we get richer, we feel no benefit.

So, to be happy, get a good job, a satisfying close relationship, and a meaningful philosophy of life. It helps to feel good about yourself, to be optimistic, stable, and healthy. Exercise, sleep well, and be grateful. Give priority to people, and realize that happiness does not result from economic success. Money prevents unhappiness; it does not buy happiness.

MONEY AND RELIGION

What has religion to do with money at work? The answer is a great deal, and it always has. The Protestant work ethic hypothesis was based on the idea that wealth creation began out of religious belief.

Religious traditions have a powerful impact on how people view their money. Consider, for instance, the Islamic rules on bank interest and usury. Consider the behavior of the Amish or indeed many Christians who still give tithes. Faith is ultimately related to values about things in this world as much as things beyond it. It dictates how people see the rich and the poor, and how people desire to acquire and spend their money.

The idea of the Protestant work ethic attempted to describe and explain the rise of personal and national capitalism based on simple but important eighteenth and nineteenth-century beliefs about work and wealth.

Economists have in fact tried to explain in their language how work ethic beliefs translated into economic force. Historically, however, there has not been in any of the world's great religions a clear distinction between work and non-work. One does not suspend faith and values on entering the workplace. Personal ethics and values are relevant in nearly all aspects of work: from the very choice of vocation itself, to the treatment of colleagues and customers.

Within the Christian tradition it appears from numerous

biblical passages that people are meant to work, to work honorably, well, and with passion (*Ecclesiastes* 3: 22). St Paul made it clear that if a person refused to work, he had no right to eat (*Thessalonians* 3: 10).

The New Testament shows fairly unambiguously that people are meant to work—to work honestly, cooperatively, and conscientiously. All work however humble or mundane is for God's glory. There is no better test of a person than the way in which he or she works. It is *how* people work, rather than what they do, that is important. It is better to do ordinary things extraordinarily well than to do extraordinary things. It is the fidelity with which work is done that is the real test. Work is a contribution owed to the community at large. Things are due from, as well as to, people at work. The parable of the laborers in the vineyard (*Matthew* 20: 1–16) suggests people have a right to work, a living wage, and reasonable working conditions.

The Christian view of pleasure is both proscriptive and prescriptive. No pleasure can be right if it is harmful to the person who indulges in it or to others, or if it becomes addictive. Any pleasure is wrong if in enjoying it the essentials of life have to take less than their proper place. Any pleasure that leads to regret is wrong. But Christianity does not deny or minimize either leisure, or pleasure, or money. Leisure and pleasure relax the mind and refresh the body.

It is generally true that the Old Testament connects goodness with prosperity, whereas wealth is associated more with affliction. From the many references to money and wealth in the Old Testament it seems wealth is seen as a gift from God, but not everything; it is essentially a secondary goal. Possession is much more a blessing than a sin, but can be a danger to character. Wealth is to be enjoyed but it is not worth making a dedicated pursuit of it. Care for the poor is the duty of the rich. To help the poor is to help God.

The New Testament is certainly clear about the danger of riches. The danger of the love of money is well recorded and well known in the story of the rich young ruler (*Mark* 10: 17–31). Poverty is not a virtue because wealth is dangerous, however. Wealth is dangerous for many reasons, partly because it can lead to arrogance, haughtiness, and snobbery (1 *Timothy* 6: 17). The value of life cannot be measured by income or wealth, which are diminishing assets. The single-minded pursuit of wealth can blind one to more important things. The parable of the rich man and Lazarus (*Luke* 16: 19–31) suggests that wealth can blind one to the needs of others as well as any sense of responsibility for their state.

The story of the cleansing of the temple by Jesus (*John* 2. 13–17) has a major moral or teaching point that it is wrong to make money out of people's credulity, trustfulness, or simple need. Christian giving (of money) through the Church is important; it should be systematic, proportionate, and universal. The New Testament is replete with messages about the dangers of wealth. It can give a false sense of independence; it can cost too much, and it can be addictive.

There are various crucial principles that the Bible teaches will save a person from the dangers of wealth:

- Is money acquired in a way that has harmed/injured no one but in fact has helped and enriched the community?
- How do we regard money—as master, enemy, servant, or friend?
- Is money spent exclusively selfishly or in the service of both self and others?

- People are more important than things; people are more important than money.
- There are times when to give money is not enough. It is impersonal giving whereas it may be that personal giving is what is required.

For all religions, certain persons, places, things, times, and social groups are collectively defined as sacred and spiritual. Sacred things are extraordinary, totally unique, set apart from, and opposed to, the profane world. Sacred objects and people can have powers of good or evil. Gifts, vacation travel, souvenirs, family photographs, pets, collections, heirlooms, homes, art, antiques: and objects associated with famous people can be regarded as existing in the realm of the sacred by many people. They are safeguarded and considered special and of spiritual value. Art and other collections become for many people sacred personal icons. Equally, heirlooms serve as mystical and fragile connections to those who are deceased. They can have more than "sentimental value," and some believe that a neglected or damaged heirloom could unleash bad luck or evil forces.

Unlike sacred objects, profane objects are interchangeable. They are valued primarily for their mundane use value. Sacred objects often lack functional use and cannot, through exchange, be converted into profane objects. Further, exchange of sacred objects for money violates their sacred status, because it brings them into inappropriate contact with the profane realm.

Money can be too sterile and ordinary to be used on special occasions. In Western societies money cannot buy brides, expiation from crimes, or (ideally) political offices. The Judaeo-Christian ethic is paradoxical on money.

People with money acquired honestly may be seen as superior, even virtuous, and removing the desire to accumulate money is condemned. Believers are called on to be altruistic, ascetic, and selfless, while simultaneously being hard working, acquisitional, and frankly capitalistic. The sacred and profane can easily get mixed up (Furnham 1990).

The sacred meaning of money is gender and class linked. Psychologists Belk and Wallendorf (1990) argue that women think of money in terms of the things into which it can be converted, while men think of it in terms of the power its possession implies. The money women deal with is profane (unless used for personal pleasure, in which case it is evil), while some of the use of money by men is sacred. Similarly, in working-class homes men traditionally gave their wages to their wives for the management of profane household needs, with a small allowance given back for individual personal pleasures, most of which were far from sacred. Yet in a middle-class house, men typically gave, and indeed sometimes still give, their wife an allowance (being a small part of their income) for collective household expenditure.

Money (an income) obtained from work that is not a source of intrinsic delight is ultimately profane, but an income derived from one's passion can be sacred. An artist can do commercial work for profane money, and the work of the soul for sacred money. From ancient Greece to twentieth-century Europe, the business of making money is often thought to be tainted. It is the activity of the *nouveaux riches*, not honorable "old money." Thus, volunteer work is sacred, while the identical job that is paid is profane. The idea of paying somebody to be a mother or home keeper may be preposterous for some because it renders the sacred duty profane. But the acts of prostitutes transform a sacred act into a formal business exchange. Some craftspeople and artists do sell their services, but at a modest, almost not going-rate, price because their aim is not to accumulate wealth but to make a reasonable income and not become burdened by their work (Belk and Wallendorf 1990).

A sacred use, for example a gift, can be "desacralized" if a person is too concerned with price. Sacralizing mechanisms usually involve the purchase of gifts and souvenirs, donations to charity, as well as the purchase of a previously sacralized object. The aim is to transform money into objects with special significance or meaning. Money-as-sacrifice and money-as-gift are clearly more sacred than money-as-commodity. Charity giving is a sacred gift only when it involves personal sacrifice and not when there is personal gain through publicity or tax relief. Money used to redeem and restore special objects (for instance, rare works of art or religious objects) is also rendered sacred.

Thus to retain all money for personal use is considered antisocial, selfish, miserly, and evil. To transform sacred money (a gift) into money (by selling it) is considered especially evil. Many people refuse to turn certain objects into money, preferring to give them away. Money violates the sacredness of objects and commoditizes them. Equally, people refuse money when offered by those who have voluntarily helped. The "good Samaritans" thereby assign their assistance to the area of the gift rather than a profane exchange. Thus a gift of help may be reciprocated by another gift.

The argument is this: the dominant view of money concentrates on its profane meaning. It is a utilitarian view that sees money transactions as impersonal and devoid of sacred money. But it becomes clear when considering the illogical behavior of collectors, gift-givers, and charity donors that money can and does have sacred meanings, both good and evil. Further, it is these sacred meanings that so powerfully influence our attitudes to money.

All religions and many secular philosophies have a great deal to say about money. The allure of the power of money and materialism is well recognized. Religious teachings with respect to money can easily influence and induce guilt about money. Perhaps part of the reason for money being a taboo topic is because so many religious teachings concern it.

CONCLUSION

Money is one of the most talked about and least talked about things on earth. Economists say it is the measure of all things but cannot itself be measured. They are wrong. If it is a metric of how we measure our worth and value, it is certainly a hot one.

Money has a moral dimension. Religions have a great deal to say about money. People can feel very guilty about money.

The media take a great deal of interest in the rich and famous. By doing so they perpetuate various myths about what money is for, what it can do, and so on. There are all sorts of reasons why money remains a taboo subject. Various theories have been put forward to explain this:

■ Rich people, who dictate etiquette, eschew discussing their money lest the poor figure out how to get it for themselves. Or because friends and relatives might want it or become envious of it.

- It is a superstition not to talk about money: It means it could be taken away.
- Boasting about money could encourage envious others to inform tax authorities.
- If money is associated with food, avoiding discussing it reduces hunger, need, greed, and vulnerability.
- If money is associated with filth in the eyes of the people, shunning discussing it can be a way of fending off feelings of shame.
- On some levels we know our attitudes to money reveal a lot about us that we would rather keep private.

Most of us like to believe that we are logical, rational, and reasonable with regard to our money. Try the following test. First complete it as honestly as you can, by answering "yes" or "no." Then try to anticipate how someone you know very well would complete it. Fill it out as you think that person should (rather than would). Get that person to do the same for you. Then compare answers. It is called meta-perception. But beware: It may herald the end of a good relationship!

1. I often buy things that I don't need or want because they are in a sale or reduced in a sale, or reduced in price.
2. I put money ahead of pleasure.
3. I sometimes buy things I don't need or want to impress people because they are the right things to have at the time.
4. Even when I have sufficient money I often feel guilty about spending money on necessities like clothes and so on.
5. Every time I make a purchase I know people are likely to be taking advantage of me.

6. I often spend money, even foolishly, on others but grudgingly on myself.
7. I often say, "I can't afford it" whether I can or not.
8. I know almost to the penny how much I have in my purse, wallet, or pocket all the time.
9. I often have difficulty in making decisions about spending money, regardless of the amount.
10. I feel compelled to argue or bargain about the cost of almost everything that I buy.
11. I insist on paying more than my (our, if married) share of the costs of a restaurant, film, and so on in order to make sure that I am not indebted to anyone.
12. If I had the choice I would prefer to be paid by the week rather than by the month.
13. I prefer to use money rather than credit cards.
14. I always know how much money I have in my savings account (bank or building society).
15. If I have some money left over at the end of the month (week) I often feel uncomfortable until it is all spent.
16. I sometimes "buy" my friendship by being very generous with those I want to like me.
17. I often feel inferior to others who have more money than myself, even when I know that they have done nothing of worth to get it.
18. I often use money as a weapon to control or intimidate those who frustrate me.
19. I sometimes feel superior to those who have less money than myself, regardless of their ability and achievements.
20. I firmly believe that money can solve all of my problems.
21. I often feel anxious and defensive when asked about my personal finances.
22. In making any purchase, for any purpose, my first consideration is cost.

23. I believe it is rude to enquire about a person's wage/salary.
24. I feel stupid if I pay more for something than a neighbor.
25. I often feel disdain for money and look down on those who have it.
26. I prefer to save money because I'm never sure when things will collapse and I'll need the cash.
27. The amount of money that I have saved is never quite enough.
28. I feel that money is the only thing that I can really count on.
29. I believe that money is the root of all evil.
30. As regards what you buy with money, I believe that you only get what you pay for.
31. I believe that money gives you considerable power.
32. My attitude towards money is very similar to that of my parents.
33. I believe that the amount of money that a person earns is closely related to his/her ability and effort.
34. I always pay bills (telephone, water, electricity, etc) promptly.
35. I often give large tips to waiters/waitresses that I like.
36. I believe that time not spent in making money is time wasted.
37. I occasionally pay restaurant/shop bills even when I think I have been overcharged because I am afraid the waiter/assistant might be angry with me.
38. I often spend money on myself when I am depressed.
39. When a person owes me money I am afraid to ask for it.
40. I don't like to borrow money from others (except banks) unless I absolutely have to.
41. I prefer not to lend people money.

42. I am better off than most of my friends think.
43. I would do practically anything legal for money if it were enough.
44. I prefer to spend money on things that last rather than on perishables like food, flowers, and so on.
45. I am proud of my financial victories—pay, riches, investments, and so on—and let my friends know about them.
46. I am worse off than most of my friends think.
47. Most of my friends have less money than I do.
48. I believe that it is generally prudent to conceal the details of my finances from friends and relatives.
49. I often argue with my partner (spouse, lover, and so on) about money.
50. I believe that people's salaries are very revealing in assessing their intelligence.
51. I believe that my present income is about what I deserve, given the job I do.
52. Most of my friends have more money than I do.
53. I believe that my present income is far less than I deserve, given the job I do.
54. I believe that I have very little control over my financial situation in terms of my power to change it.
55. Compared with most people that I know, I believe that I think about money much more than they do.
56. I worry about my finances much of the time.
57. I often fantasize about money and what I could do with it.
58. I very rarely give beggars or drunks money when they ask for it.
59. I am proud of my ability to save money.
60. In my country, money is how we compare each other.

References

Baker, G.P.; Jenson, M.C.; Murphy, K.J. (1988) Compensation and incentives: practice vs. theory. *Journal of Finance,* **43** (3), pp. 593–616.

Behrend, H. (1988) The wage–work bargain. *Managerial and Decision Economics,* Special issue, pp. 51–7.

Belk, R.W.; Wallendorf, M. (1990) The sacred meanings of money. *Journal of Economic Psychology,* **11**, pp. 35–67.

Belsky, G.; Gilovich, T. (1999) *Why Smart People Make Big Money Mistakes— And How to Correct Them.* New York: Simon and Schuster.

Bodnar, J. (1993). *Dr Tightwad's Money-Smart Kids.* New York: Random House.

Cappelli, P. & Chauvin, K (1991) An inter-plant test of efficiency wage arguments. *Quarterly Journal of Economics,* **103**, pp. 769–87.

Csikszentmihalyi, M. (1990) *Flow.* London: HarperCollins.

Deci, E.L.; Koestner, R.; Ryan, R.M. (1999) A meta-analytic review of experiments examining the effects of extrinsic reward on intrinsic motivation. *Psychological Bulletin,* **125**, pp. 627–68.

Diener, E.; Diener M.; Diener, C. (1995) Factors predicting the subjective well-being of nations. *Journal of Personality and Social Psychology,* **69**, pp. 851–64.

Eisenberger, R.; Rhoades, L.; Cameron, J. (1999) Does pay for performance increase or decrease perceived self-determination and intrinsic motivation? *Journal of Personality and Social Psychology,* **77** (5), pp. 1026–40.

Forman, N. (1987) *Mind Over Money.* Toronto: Doubleday.

Furnham, A. (1990) *The Protestant Work Ethic: The Psychology of work related beliefs and behaviours.* London: Routledge.

Furnham, A.; Argyle, M. (1998) *The Psychology of Money.* London: Routledge.

Gardner, J.; Oswald, A. (2001) Does money buy happiness? A longitudinal study using data on windfalls. Royal Economic Society Annual Conference.

Goldberg, H.; Lewis, R. (1978) *Money Madness.* London: Springwood Books.

Hilton, D. (1998) *Psychology and the City.* London: CSFI.

Inglehart, R. (1990) *Culture Shift in Advanced Industrial Society.* Princeton, NJ: Princeton University Press.

Jenkins, D.G.Jr.; Gupta, N.; Mitra, A.; Shaw, J.D. (1998) Are financial incentives related to performance? A meta-analytic review of empirical research. *Journal of Applied Psychology,* **83** (5), pp.777–87.

Kohn, A. (1993) *Punished by Rewards: The trouble with gold stars, incentive plans, A's, praise and other bribes.* New York: Houghton Mifflin.

Lea, S.E.G.; Webley, P. (1999) Money as tool, money as drug: The psychology of a strong incentive. Unpublished paper. University of Exeter.

Maslow, A.H. (1954) *Motivation and Personality.* New York: Harper.

Matthews, A.M. (1991) *If I Think About MONEY so Much, Why Can't I Figure it out? Understanding and overcoming your money complex.* London: Summit Books.

Myers, D. (1992) *The Pursuit of Happiness.* New York: Avon Books.

Ott, J. (2001) Did the market depress happiness in the US? *Journal of Happiness Studies,* **2**, pp. 433–43.

Smith, A. (1937) *An Inquiry into the Nature and Causes of the Wealth of Nations.* New York: Modern Library (original work published in 1776).

Toynbee, P. (2003) Money and happiness. *Guardian,* March 7.

Wilson, V. (1999). *The Secret Life of Money: Exposing the private parts of personal money.* London: Allen & Unwin.

Wiseman, T. (1974) *The Money Motive: A study of obsession.* London: Hutchinson.